THE
DOG FOOD
DETECTIVE

THE
DOG FOOD
DETECTIVE

HOW TO CHOOSE
THE BEST DOG FOOD

(Find the right food
for your best friend
and your budget)

CRAIG WEINDLING

Published by Smiley Dog Press, Bothell, WA

Cover Design: Trisha Cupra, Quokka Creative

Illustrations: Philip G. Riggs

Interior Design: Nick Zelinger, NZ Graphics

Editor: Lizabet Nix, WORDcredible!

ISBN: 978-0-9916304-0-0

Library of Congress Control Number: 2014908206

1. Dogs 2. Dogs- Food 3. Dogs- Nutrition 4. Pet Food

First Edition

Printed in the United States of America

He is your friend, your partner, your defender, your dog.
You are his life, his love, his leader.
He will be yours, faithful and true, to the last beat of his heart.
You owe it to him to be worthy of such devotion.
— Unknown

CONTENTS

Preface: Just Another Pet Food Book? 1

Introduction: The Scene of the Crime. 5

How to Use This Book. 9

Step 1: Sniff Out the Evidence 13
    The Initial Briefing 15
    Follow the Money 21
    Eliminate Distractions 27
    Identify Special Needs 33
    Review Your Results 41
    Summary: Sniff Out the Evidence. 42

Step 2: Consider the Culprits 45
    Spot the Suspects. 47
    Interrogate the Ingredients. 57
    Expose the Scam of Splitting 67
    Cross-Examine Meat, Meal and By-Products 75
    Summary: Consider the Culprits 85

Step 3: Engage the Hidden Players 87
    Employ the Informant 89
    Review the Forensics of Guaranteed Analysis. 97
    Recognize Tips, Tricks and Traps of Labels. 105
    Summary: Engage the Hidden Players. 117

Cracking the Case 119
    Closing Arguments. 121
    Afterword: Render Your Verdict. 127

Appendix 1: Dog Food Detective System™ Exercises 131

Appendix 2: Supporting References 149

Bibliography & Resource List. 157

Preface

Just Another Pet Food Book?

Trust, but verify.

This phrase was often used in the context of dealing with the former Soviet Union. It was made famous by a world figure. Think you know which one?

And what in the world does "trust, but verify" have to do with dog food?

Let me say this up front:

I'm not a huge fan of dry dog foods.

Granted, some are better than others. But when compared to fresh, whole foods, even the "best" dry dog foods are dead, processed, and biologically deficient.

There. I said it. I feel better now.

So why trust a dry dog food cycnic to help choose your food?

Simple.

Most of us feed dry dog food. And I did, too.

When I first switched to a better dry food, I was astonished at how quickly my dog's appearance and energy improved. Over the years, nothing has been more gratifying than helping our clients see the same type of improvements with their dogs.

So even though I prefer fresh food, there are huge benefits that come with choosing a good dry dog food. That's what I'd like to share with you in this book—how to find that good food. But to do that, a few questions must be answered.

What's the best dog food?

This is one of the most common questions I've been asked in more than 20 years in the pet food business. I have the same answer for everyone:

There is no such thing as the *best* dog food.

But there is a simple way to choose the best food for *your* dog. And I'd bet a fresh marrow bone that you'd like to make the "best" choice for yourself, rather than rely on the advice of others.

Now you can, with the help of this book.

There's no reason to let others choose your dog's food

Your needs are different from mine. The best food for you reflects *your* preferences and has nothing to do with mine. It doesn't really matter what anyone else likes if their choices don't meet your needs.

Most of us feed dry dog food because the convenience and cost just can't be beat. I used to feed Purina Hi-Protein dog food because it was, you know, *High Protein*. Protein is good, so *high* protein had to be better, right?

That was a long, long, time ago. What a difference a bit of education makes.

We all have to start somewhere

There's no need to repeat my mistakes or rely on what other people say. I believe you can benefit from my research, observation and guidance of pet parents over the past 20+ years.

I have no interest in pushing a particular brand or style of food on you. With just a few common sense tips, many of which you may already know, you'll be on your way to seeing dog food differently.

Earlier, I said I have the same answer for everyone when asked about the best food. That's not entirely true. I have the same questions for everyone. The answers are often different.

So for your dog's sake, understand what you're feeding. Know what to seek out and what to avoid. Be curious. Skeptical. Informed.

Don't be a pet food victim

The pet food industry uses creative advertising to win the hearts and minds of consumers. Make them earn your trust. Protect yourself by understanding how to see through the hype and find the truth.

The mission of this book is to help you recognize and overcome your confusion about pet food choices. Whether it's conflicting advice, an overwhelming number of options, or lack of pet food knowledge, this guide can help.

In a few very short chapters, we'll journey through the world of Captain K. Nyne, our infamous Dog Food Detective. We'll share some stories along the way, and identify a cast of characters to acknowledge and avoid.

You will soon see pet food differently

A wise man once said, "And so it is with anything in life. If you learn to see things, you see them. Otherwise, your brain just blithely ignores them as if they don't exist."

This journey will empower you to make informed choices. You'll have developed a system of verification.

Trust, but verify

Ronald Reagan may have made this a household phrase. But it's not his quote.

It is taken from a Russian proverb, believed to have been first uttered by a former head of the Soviet secret police.

Trust, but verify. Valuable advice which guides us along the journey to becoming a Dog Food Detective.

Turn the page to learn how.

Introduction:
The Scene of the Crime

Sizing up the situation

Why is it that Sherlock Holmes and the Pink Panther almost always manage to crack their cases? Despite using completely different methods, both enjoy great success. What do they have in common?

The answer lies in the system

Sherlock's methodical, logical system can easily be adapted to most situations. Inspector Clouseau has a different "system." He bumbles about, benefiting from coincidence and the common sense of others before arriving at his conclusions.

Despite different personalities, each follows a proven system to produce a consistent, successful result.

Whether questioning a witness or suspect, examining evidence, or drawing a conclusion, it is the system which helps to crack a case.

Where do you turn for help?

It's easy to be confused by the variety of choices found in the pet food aisle. As nice as it would be to have Mr. Holmes choose the best food for our pets, it's not really necessary. We can employ our own system. There's no need for outside help.

By following the simple steps of this system, you gain the confidence to trust yourself. No one will protect your interests better than you do. Not a store employee or a manufacturer's rep. Not even a trusted friend.

You will always be your own best advocate. All that's needed is some basic background, a bit of curiosity, and a simple way to connect the dots.

Those dots are the three simple steps of the Dog Food Detective System™.

What is the Dog Food Detective System?

The Dog Food Detective (DFD) System makes a seemingly complex jumble of competing dog foods understandable. It simplifies the process of dog food evaluation into three easy steps. No more pet food confusion!

The three steps of the DFD System include:

1. Sniff out the evidence by eliminating distractions
2. Identify and interrogate the usual ingredient suspects
3. Use informants to uncover disguises and reveal the true cost of a food

The DFD System simplifies your choices

The three steps of the DFD System quickly become second nature. You decide what is most important and the System guides you through the options.

The DFD System goes beyond reading the Ingredient List. It shows you how to quickly uncover misinformation and remove confusion. There's no need to memorize complicated formulas, keep track of points or delve deeply into the molecular structure of nutrients to use the System.

Whatever your priority, from budget to quality, the DFD System helps you make the best choices for your dog's food quickly and easily.

The system makes you a Dog Food Detective

A Dog Food Detective can glance at a bag of pet food and objectively assess its quality and value in less than a minute.

As a DFD, you'll easily compare foods without the distractions of misleading packaging or marketing claims. You'll understand why a less expensive bag of food may actually cost you more. Along the way, you'll discover why some foods that present themselves as fresh and healthy are actually neither.

A DFD sees through deception and coded information. Mistaken identity of foods becomes a thing of the past. The skills you learn will serve you and your dog for a lifetime.

Why should you accept the DFD System approach?

No single approach is right for everyone. Skepticism is a useful tool, and one that's encouraged as you implement the DFD System.

Embrace your skepticism at the beginning of this journey. You will quickly discover whether this is the right approach for you. Of course, advice is always available from friends and pet shops. As a DFD, you'll better understand whether this advice is useful or not.

Thousands of pet owners have benefited from the DFD System. It is your simple and fast path to become a DFD.

Begin your journey to become a DFD

Imagine standing in the midst of that pet food aisle enjoying the colors, designs and variety in front of you. You're no longer intimidated by the range of options. You know exactly how to narrow down your choices to those few foods that offer precisely what you're after. Sherlock would be proud.

Come join us on a lighthearted look into becoming a Dog Food Detective. Begin on the next page and follow through to the end, or choose your own path through the book.

You'll find Case File excerpts and Evidence Archives to support each step of the System. A few words from Captain K at the end of each chapter will help refresh your memory. Closing Arguments offer a final quick review of the System.

However you choose to travel through the material, a diploma awaits at the conclusion of your trip.

Let's get started!

How to Use This Book:
Master the Dog Food Detective System™

You're about to meet and master the three simple steps of the Dog Food Detective System™.

Will this System teach you everything you need to know?

Absolutely not! Learning is a lifetime adventure. The purpose of this book is to help you begin to see dog food differently.

This book gives you a solid foundation

The Dog Food Detective System guides you through a simple, universal approach to choosing dog food. Based on the needs of both you and your pet, it shows how to cut through distractions and concentrate on the essentials.

Here's what you can expect

The DFD System removes the mystery and confusion you encounter when looking at dog food. You may already review Ingredient Lists, Guaranteed Analysis, and other label information. But how well do you understand what you see? Flip through the Table of Contents before you decide to move on. There just may be some steps you've missed.

Your level of understanding will be your best guide to the use of this book. You may find yourself already following much of the advice in

Step 1. You may choose to spend a few hours with each section. Or you may buzz through from start to finish in one sitting.

Any approach is just fine. The book is designed to remove common obstacles which can sidetrack you from reaching your goal: gaining the confidence to make your own decisions based on facts and common sense.

Some examples appear throughout the book

 Within each section this icon introduces excerpts from *Captain K's Case Files*. These real-life situations help illustrate a specific point of the System. You may find some that mirror your own concerns

 *Evidence Archives* have their own icon and are found at the end of some chapters. These examples go a bit deeper in support of the material presented. If you're just starting out, you won't miss much if you skip these during your first reading. But they will add to your understanding as you're mastering the System.

You'll also find a summary and graphic at the end of each Section. These will give you a quick reminder of where we've been, and where we're going.

Appendix #1 contains some exercises to show you the System in action. The pricing and Ingredient Lists used in these examples are taken from existing pet foods.

Why don't we name the foods cited in this book?

You can find the names of all foods used in examples listed in Appendix #2. To avoid any bias during our training, those names were kept out of the body of the book. We all have our favorites and our failures. The problem is that they are moving targets.

Some brands are only available regionally. Others change their formulas like we change clothes.

If you're eager to know the names of foods cited in an example, refer to the Appendix. Just keep in mind that these foods may have changed their approach for better or worse. Your DFD training will easily tell you which when you look at an actual label.

Along the way questions are sure to arise

Your questions should be answered by the time you reach the end of your training.

If not, feel free to contact us at Dog-Food-Detective.com.

The Dog Food Detective System addresses most common concerns with dry food. As circumstances change, you'll find the System easily adapts. If you encounter a situation that appears to defy the System, please share it with the rest of the DFD community on the site. We'll all benefit from what you discover.

Your detective training does not need to stop when you reach the end of this book. Visit Dog-Food-Detective.com often to see what others are asking. Add your voice to the discussion!

Step 1

Sniff out the Evidence

The Initial Briefing
Follow the Money
Eliminate Distractions
Identify Special Needs
Review Your Results

The Initial Briefing of the Dog Food Detective System™

We all have to start somewhere.

In February of 2012, a $25 billion settlement was announced in a case against five mortgage companies in the United States. It began with the filing of a single lawsuit.

In 1998, the Attorneys General of 46 states settled with major tobacco companies for more than 200 billion dollars. The case began with a solitary lawsuit filed by the Attorney General of Mississippi.

In 1996, Erin Brockovich, a legal clerk with no formal law school education, successfully led a civil lawsuit which resulted in a $333 million settlement for the residents of Hinkley, CA.

Few people would have imagined these outcomes. The resources of the giant corporations involved created overwhelming obstacles. A single person, armed with simple facts, curiosity and a clear goal, began each of these cases. Those individuals prevailed, despite overwhelming odds.

You can overcome the odds as well.

It's been said that everyone loves an underdog

We may feel like an underdog facing insurmountable challenges as we begin a pet food investigation. But we are not alone in this case. Our trusted Dog Food Detective System™ will guide us through the maze of options from start to finish and clarify our choices.

Teri beamed as she walked through the door of the pet shop, followed by a hesitant mixed breed dog at the end of her leash. "I just adopted Koko from the shelter, and they gave me enough food for tonight," she said, holding out a bag of kibble. "Can I get some more of this?"

The clerk asked what kind of food she wanted and motioned towards the back wall. Teri's smile faded as she saw the dozens of choices stacked floor to ceiling. "It's just dog food, isn't it? I guess I'll just pick some up on my way home when I get bread and milk. I don't know how to choose."

Our best choices come from setting a clear goal and ignoring any misleading distractions that pop up along the way. The DFD System begins by examining budget and personal preferences. This reduces distractions to help keep us clearly focused on one objective.

The goal is to find the best food for our pet

Ask any number of pet lovers about the best dog food, and you'll receive different answers from each. That's to be expected since we all have different priorities.

To find the best dog food for our pet, we'll examine what is truly most important to our case. Our investigation begins with three simple considerations that help eliminate distractions:

1. Budget
2. Personal Preference
3. Special Needs

Let's follow the money and begin by examining our budget.

Captain K says:
"*Never fear! The Dog Food Detective System will guide you through the maze.*
It's just like solving any other case.
Let's get started with the first step: Follow the money!"

From the "Initial Briefing" Evidence Archive

Some dog food recommendations make sense, and others do not. It's up to you to decide what best serves your interests. In the first steps of this journey, you may not feel comfortable making these decisions. By the end of the book, you will!

Eric sat down at the table, looked over his shoulder and shook his head in disbelief. "That's absolutely appalling. I can't believe what I just heard."

Captain K glanced behind Eric and noticed a small group of people clustered around a local breeder with a dog by her side.

"Did you know that a Breeder's Contract can void the health guarantee of a puppy unless a particular food is fed?" Eric asked.

Well, yes. Some breeders, for a variety of reasons, will require that purchasers of their puppies feed a particular brand of food. Some require a raw diet. Others require a specific brand of lower quality kibble.

And if you don't particularly care for the food named in the contract? In most cases, deviating from the specified food releases the breeder from the contract. If the puppy becomes sick, you can't make a health-related claim because you didn't dispense the agreed upon food.

The reasons breeders specify foods in their contracts can range from best intentions to corporate sponsorship. Some large pet food companies offer sweetheart deals to breeders who feed or recommend their food. Some veterinarian clinics participate in similar deals. While this may seem unethical, it's a common business practice.

Other breeders are raw food advocates, and insist that their litters continue to be fed in this manner. As wonderful as this feeding method is, it should be for the new pet parent to decide. It is highly unusual to find a similar requirement when adopting from a shelter or rescue group.

There's nothing wrong with a breeder making a recommendation of what, or how, to feed. It's quite a different matter when that becomes a requirement of sale.

When we understand how to make informed choices, our dogs will benefit. We should have the final say over what our dogs eat, not a third party.

And we will begin to do so by following the money.

Follow the Money:
How Setting a Budget Narrows the Field

Let's borrow a cliché from our beloved friend, the used car salesman: "How much are you looking to spend?"

Don't you just love that question? It invokes a reflex that immediately raises our defenses. Do we spin around and walk away, or snidely retort "as little as possible?"

Why start with budget before knowing what good food costs?

There will always be a more expensive food. There will always be a "better" food option. But these have nothing to do with choosing the best food for you.

You want to buy the best food that fits your budget and addresses your specific needs. A bit of questioning can reveal those needs and narrow your options.

Are you training sled dogs to work in the Arctic tundra or will you have a companion pet in the city? Do you want to feed dry food or a homemade raw diet? Are you spending 30 weekends of the year doing agility work or simply playing in the park and walking daily?

No single food can possibly address all these circumstances. It bears repeating: there is no such thing as "the best" dog food. We're after what's best for *you*.

Penny did a double take when she heard her sister was spending over $100 each month for dog food. "Dog food is dog food, isn't it?" she asked. "I don't even spend half that much for my dog, and he's doing just fine."

Penny has no good reason to increase her budget. The food she's using came highly recommended by a friend, and she's satisfied with her results. Until she has more information, there's no reason to change what's working.

How do you set a budget?

Here's where we must take a leap of faith and plow through some early distractions. At this point, it's not necessary to settle on a budget number. Rather, it's more important to identify a *range of pricing*. As we consider product options, a range of prices from high to low will be revealed.

Start by asking yourself some simple questions: Do you want a food for a particular life stage or lifestyle? Will an Adult or All Life Stages formula work or do you prefer Puppy or Senior?

Sticking with general guidelines like these begins to narrow the field. For example, often there's little difference between an Adult formula and an All Life Stages formula. If you're shopping for a puppy, you can look at Puppy and All Life Stage foods, but may want to ignore Adult and Senior.

Within the same brand, a Puppy formula will usually be slightly more expensive than the Adult, All Life Stages or Senior formula.

Pricing will vary depending on where you shop

To help keep focused on the goal, develop your range of prices from one retail outlet for Step 1 of this investigation. You will duplicate a certain amount of effort if you shop multiple locations at this stage.

Be sure to develop your price range using similar size bags. Most foods are available in Small (3-7 pound), Medium (10-20 pound) and Large (24-40 pound) bags. The actual weight of each size may vary between brands, but that's not overly important for our purpose in Step 1. Stick with one of these three sizes to get an initial price range.

We've got a price range, now what?

Becoming familiar with your price range is an important clue at the start of this investigation. It begins to establish a frame of reference to work within. If our appealing options range in price from $35-$60, we may be less likely to consider a $70 bag of food. We'll also most likely skip the $25 bag of food at the low end of the range.

Perhaps you're thinking it's rather silly to settle on a price range before understanding more about what you're buying. Certainly that's a valid point. But we start with budget because it's an important question for almost everyone. By first identifying a price range, we lay the groundwork for Steps 2 and 3 of the DFD System. If you prefer to begin by considering your personal preferences, that works just as well!

Budget and personal preferences are closely linked

You could begin instead by pondering some personal preferences, as we do on the next page, and then move to budget. Either way, the result will be the same.

Poof! The potential number of food choices has been cut in half. All of a sudden, choosing a dog food doesn't seem nearly as overwhelming as it did a few moments ago. So let's narrow things down a bit further by looking at those personal preferences.

Captain K says:
"This is my kind of budgeting!
Find a range from cheap to spendy and call it good.
Next we play with personal preferences."

From the "Follow the Money" Evidence Archive

AAFCO (Association of American Feed Control Officials) is responsible for ingredient definitions, labeling guidelines and minimum nutrition standards for each type of pet food.

While AAFCO has oversight authority on what may and may not be used in pet foods, it has "no overriding legal authority" to enforce its own regulations.

AAFCO is an advisory board, made up of members of state and federal government agencies, and is lobbied by pet food manufacturers. It is not a government agency, although all members must be government officials.

Pet food industry lobbyists may serve on AAFCO working groups, or as advisers to AAFCO committees, but cannot vote or make motions in these meetings.

AAFCOs guidelines are intended to ensure that a food meets minimum nutritional standards, based on either feeding trials or laboratory analysis.

You've most likely seen the phrase "formulated to meet the nutrient levels established by the AAFCO nutrient profiles" on dog food packaging. AAFCO has set nutritional standards and guidelines for different life stage formulas – Puppy, Adult, Senior, Overweight and All Life Stages. The standards mandate a range of values for the Guaranteed Analysis Panel, as well as vitamin and mineral content in a formula.

A pet food that does not meet AAFCO standards may not display the AAFCO nutritional adequacy statement.

When a food does not meet these standards, it is not considered "complete and balanced." It can still be sold and labeled for "supplemental or intermittent feeding", or carry no nutritional claims at all.

A Dog Food Detective is aware of AAFCO's role in pet food, and understands which guidelines can be misleading. This awareness helps cut through much of the marketing clutter that is a major source of distraction.

Eliminate Distractions:
How Personal Preferences Clarify Our Case

Paper or plastic? Cash, check or charge? Would you like fries with that? Hardly a day goes by without facing some type of simple decision based on our personal preferences.

Our choice of pet food also begins with simple decisions based on personal preference. Perhaps a friend recommended you look at, or stay away from, a particular line of food. Maybe you have fond memories of, or had a bad experience with a previous brand. Your current budget may have to dictate what you can consider.

Self-interrogation reveals personal preferences

Let's put ourselves on the witness stand for a moment to examine our remaining options. Personal preferences will help remove distractions in our food choices so we can concentrate on what we truly value.

- Would you like to feed a chicken-based food?
- Do you cringe when you think of feeding lamb?
- Have you been attracted by a particular advertisement?
- Will you be feeding the same food or do you prefer to rotate formulas?
- Large bags or small? Breed specific? Grain-free?

Personal preferences answer these questions

We are no longer distracted by foods that didn't survive the "personal preference cut." This further narrows the options within our budget range and brings us slightly closer to our goal. Progress!

We can dig a bit deeper at this point, or solicit an outside opinion. A second opinion can serve as a cross-examination of sorts. It will either confirm or complicate our initial findings.

If you want a second opinion, seek out the counsel of a trustworthy, independent pet shop. But beware: some shops may put their own interests ahead of yours.

Walking into the shop, Peter thought he wanted to know a bit more about three brands of food before setting his budget. After a 40-minute conversation with a salesperson, he got the distinct impression he was being pushed toward one specific brand.

"Why are you recommending this one?" Peter asked. By digging deeper, Peter found out that the store was running a promotion on the recommended food. Whoever sold the most of that brand by the end of the month would receive a pair of free movie tickets.

Paul arrived at the same shop, having chosen to confine his search to moderately active adult formulas costing under $50. Less than five minutes later, he had a short list of four possibilities and a range of pricing, including the formula that was being pushed on Peter. Paul immediately narrowed his list to three when he learned about the promotional food recommendation.

When making suggestions, a salesperson should ask about your preferences and keep your budget range in mind. Rather than accepting their information as fact, ask why they are making a particular recommendation.

Asking questions helps ensure that the shop's suggestions are a response to your needs, not what results in the best profit margin for them. While it can be good to know what others think, it is not a good substitute for our own choices.

The ultimate goal is to make our own choices

If we accept a suggestion before fully understanding the underlying reasons, it can stall our progress. When we choose a food based on our own preferences, we have a deeper understanding about why the choice is made. This understanding allows for easier fine-tuning as future adjustments are considered.

What works well for one dog may, or may not, work well for another. A lamb-based food is not "better" than a chicken-based food. A grain-free food is not necessarily better for your dog. You won't know for certain until your dog eats a particular formula. All dogs are different.

Remember, we're still in the preliminary stages of this investigation. If you are more comfortable settling your personal preferences before setting your budget, go right ahead. Either way, we end up with the same short list of possibilities. And our short list may be about to get shorter (and more specific) as we consider special needs.

Captain K says:

"*Narrowing down food options is simpler than you may think. Actually, it's just as simple as asking yourself a few targeted questions:*

'What are my personal preferences and budget?'

Then watch the distractions disappear!"

From the "Eliminate Distractions" Evidence Archive:

Trisha was the perfect representative to voice a common question: "I know there are 'better' foods out there, but why are they better? They cost an arm and a leg. My dog looks bright-eyed and bushy-tailed, and doesn't get sick. Why should I bother changing the dog food or spend more money?"

Well, perhaps you shouldn't change. What you could do is understand whether a change would result in a positive benefit. It comes down to a matter of health, and wanting to eliminate as many potential dangers as possible. The outward appearance of a dog is often an excellent reflection of inner health. Up to a point.

When your dog's coat is dry, brittle or shedding a lot, it can be a sign of illness, or a compromised immune system. Bad breath, watery eyes, and stinky skin are all easy to spot. In many cases these symptoms can be addressed by an improvement in diet.

When there are no outward signs, why bother to change things up? We hear about centenarian smokers, heavy drinkers who outlive their teetotaler friends and the 105-year-old woman who credits bacon for her longevity.

Do these examples prove that potentially destructive habits don't matter? On the contrary, they are seen as exceptions to the belief that a healthy diet equals a longer, healthier life.

When a dog eats properly, it is much better equipped to battle disease and recover from injury. As in humans, proper diet supports

31

the immune system, major organs, bones, teeth, overall physical and mental health. A healthy diet allows for better weight control, which in turn reduces the chances of muscle, skeletal or joint issues.

No one can definitively pinpoint the exact measurement of nutrients that every dog requires to maintain ideal health. This is why AAFCO has developed its minimum nutritional guidelines which all "complete and balanced" diets use as a guide. These standards are woefully inadequate in some cases, and overly generous in others. They serve as an average guide.

One thing everyone can agree upon is the need for certain essential nutrients to be provided by diet. Many nutrients are produced or stored during the digestive process. Those that are not must be provided in a dog's daily food.

A list of AAFCO's recommended guidelines, including the essential and non-essential nutrients, appears in the Nutritional Reference Bonus Report.

This is interesting information, but not particularly important to a Dog Food Detective in training. Most of these nutritional questions resolve themselves through the application of the DFD System.

Becoming sidetracked by nutrient requirements at this early stage compromises our investigation with unnecessary distractions. However, nutrient requirements may become more of a factor as we now look at special needs.

Identify Special Needs:
Separate Special Needs from Personal Preferences

The special needs that the DFD System addresses are limited to age, weight, food sensitivities or intolerances. Addressing these needs further narrows our options quite nicely.

Sometimes there's confusion when the discussion turns to food allergies, ingredient sensitivities and intolerances. Allergies and other more serious medical conditions may be best diagnosed and treated by your vet. However, most sensitivities and intolerances can be addressed with the diet choices made for your pet.

Food allergies in dogs are relatively rare

It is far more common for dogs to have an ingredient *sensitivity* rather than an allergy. The two terms are often used interchangeably, but are medically different. Knowing the difference helps us steer clear of potential traps and overly expensive solutions.

A food *allergy* normally causes a dog's immune system to immediately overreact. This can be quite dangerous as the immune system goes on the attack for what it considers to be an invader. Allergies normally produce intense and immediate symptoms, and can affect multiple organs.

Most food allergies result from ingesting a protein source that triggers an immune system response. A DFD does not need to be overly concerned about the scientific distinction between immunoglobulin and histamines. An allergy can usually be diagnosed with skin or blood testing through your veterinarian or lab if other approaches are unsuccessful.

Ingredient sensitivities are more common than allergies

Sensitivity reactions, while unpleasant, are often less immediate and less severe than allergies. They can also develop over time. Some symptoms of sensitivities can be similar to those of an allergic response.

An ingredient sensitivity or intolerance is usually not as critical as an allergy since it does not trigger a full-blown immune system response.

Sensitivities usually result from a dog not being able to tolerate or process a particular ingredient properly. Common symptoms of sensitivity include itching, digestive issues, loose stool, hair loss and recurring ear infections. Eliminating the offending ingredient is the best course of action. But sensitivities also can be a stubborn mystery to solve.

When a dog shows signs of an ingredient sensitivity or intolerance, the first suspect is, once again, a food's protein source. If the current food is chicken-based, eliminating chicken-based foods from consideration is the first course of action.

Grains are often accused, but rarely convicted

Some dogs can have difficulty digesting grains such as wheat and corn. Others thrive with whole grains as part of their diets. If we suspect grains may be a problem, it's easy enough to avoid them. We simply confine our options to grain-free formulas.

Grain sensitivities are often unfairly blamed for problems. Grains make a convenient scapegoat since a meat protein is far more likely to trigger symptoms than a grain.

When using a grain-free formula to identify a "suspect" grain ingredient, keep the meat protein source the same. This will help determine if the grain ingredient is truly the problem. If the sensitivity does not subside, change the protein source.

Some grain-free formulas are limited ingredient diets

Avoiding or selecting a specific meat protein and other ingredients may lead us to consider "limited ingredient diets." These foods may, or may not, include grains. These formulas have a very short ingredient list, which can make it easier to isolate the cause of a sensitivity issue.

Limited ingredient diets are available from a variety of manufacturers. Some can be used as "elimination diets". These severely restrict or target specific ingredients which we suspect to be problematic. When addressing food sensitivities, these formulas can be useful when we fully understand what the ingredient label tells us. The same holds true for other early stage special needs.

Ruby was pondering whether she should take her veterinarian's advice and find a puppy formula for her new wriggly furbaby. Her adult dog was doing very well on a grain-free adult formula, and the idea of trying to keep two foods separate was less than appealing.

"Baby wolves in the wild eat the same thing as their parents, don't they?" she reasoned with herself. By feeding an All Life Stages formula she was able to simplify her food choices and both dogs are thriving.

How important are "designer" formulas?

Pet food companies formulate foods for specific ages, breeds, seasons and even coat colors. This would lead us to believe that all of these formulations address special needs. Is this more marketing than science? It can be if we allow ourselves to become distracted by these types of special foods, which are really just personal preferences.

Most adult foods are formulated for all life stages. This means they have been developed to provide adequate nutrition for puppies, adults, and senior dogs.

These days, with advances in dog food nutrition like All Life Stages foods, it is less important to select a Puppy food or Senior food based solely on age. It's more important to consider the condition, activity level and weight of your dog when narrowing options.

A peppy puppy can certainly benefit from a good quality Puppy formula. A sedate senior may maintain proper weight when fed a Senior formula. Both of these furkids may also do just fine on an Adult food formulated for all life stages. Personal preference and environment, rather than special needs, determine which formula is appropriate.

The same holds true for breed-specific formulas. There's both science and marketing behind them. It's far more important to consider the ingredients in the bag than the claims for a specific breed that appear on the label.

What about weight control?

An overweight or underweight dog can benefit from a food which takes its condition into account. For dogs with weight management needs, it can be helpful to know the fat and protein content of our options. This is one of the few situations where Guaranteed Analysis numbers can be useful. We'll look closer at Guaranteed Analysis in Step 3.

The quality of a food has as much, or more of an effect on weight control as those Guaranteed Analysis numbers. Weight issues can often be more easily managed with a better quality food because of its higher digestibility.

Stay on track with what you want

When your dog has known food sensitivities or allergies, many options containing suspect ingredients are immediately ruled out.

This eliminates a huge range of possibilities that are no longer appropriate.

When shopping for an underweight or overweight dog, our options can be narrowed to address these needs. If we decide we want a Puppy or Senior formula, we can limit ourselves to those options only.

Medical conditions such as allergies or disease may introduce a prescription food as part of a treatment approach. The DFD System can still be used with prescription foods. In these cases, the System must be balanced with the changing goal of management or cure for the condition. When the condition is under control, apply the System once again with pet store options.

Special needs are just that, special. It's possible to have none at the moment, but discover some as we learn more about our dogs and their diets. Special needs may also arise as our dogs age. The DFD System allows our approach to be adjusted when needed.

Captain K says:

"Yes, of course you're special! But does your dog really have special needs?

Cleverly contrived marketing hype can easily throw you off track.

Take a clue from your dog and don't complicate things unnecessarily."

From the "Special Needs" Evidence Archive:

A typical tale from one pet parent who opted to address special needs with diet:

"Minnie never had her allergies tested. One vet wanted to do it (and get thousands of dollars in the process). I went to a different vet with a holistic approach (part science, part homeopathy and nutritional-oriented), and he was the one that helped control Minnie's issues in a far more cost-effective way.

He never tried to sell me a certain brand of dog food. He was the one who gave me the recipes for Minnie's home cooked meals. Sadly he's retired now, but I trusted him far more than any other vets who try to sell certain (nasty) brands of kibble.

Minnie gets two kinds of kibble – they are both super-premium brands. I don't have kids – Minnie is my spoilt fur child – so I'm happy to spend money on her, but I don't like vets trying to con me."

It can be challenging to know when to trust, and when to question, the advice you're getting from so-called experts. The truth is that the traditional veterinarian curriculum does not spend much time on nutrition. They can't – there is so much other ground to cover that nutrition often gets short shrift.

Much of the pet food nutrition curriculum in veterinary schools has been developed with assistance from major pet food manufacturers.

More than one-third of the contributors listed in the definitive textbook, *Small Animal Clinical Nutrition*, have ties to pet food or pharmaceutical companies.

It is encouraging that the industry is involved in developing the nutritional curriculum, although there is evidence that the resulting courses are often skewed toward industry interests.

Just think how your doctor's perspective would be affected if med school training were primarily based on information provided by the pharmaceutical industry, rather than objective medical science!

Even with dog food, our opinions are easily swayed until we know what information to trust. Our preliminary investigation has eliminated some suspects, while closing in on others.

Review Your Results:
Closing in on the Suspects

Our preliminary investigation is now complete.

We've set a budget range and pondered personal preferences. We've seen which special needs truly exist and which can be ignored. Completion of Step 1 greatly reduces confusion by narrowing our range of choices.

Can this step eliminate good options?

We're now left with a lineup of foods which are better suited to our needs. By eliminating distractions that are not worthy of our attention, we can take a closer look at the remaining suspects.

Our circumstances may change over time, causing us to shift our initial budget range or preferences. When this happens, our list can be adjusted to reflect the changes.

Step 1 of the System allows for easy adjustments

Any changes to budget, personal preferences or special needs quickly identifies a new targeted range of suspects by the same process of elimination.

It's far easier to confine questioning to a few qualified suspects than to interrogate the entire population. We can move on to Step 2 with confidence that our preliminary investigation is on target. We are closing in on the suspects. But first let's summarize what we've covered in Step 1.

Summary: Step 1
Sniff Out the Evidence

So, here we are at the end of Step 1. Let's summarize before moving on to more meaty things in Step 2.

- Always remember the goal: find the best food for your dog.

- The best food will be based on your personal preferences, including budget.

- Set a budget range based on personal preferences. Do you want to seek out, or avoid a particular brand or meat protein? Do you prefer a specialized formula like grain-free or breed specific?

- Be consistent when pricing bag sizes, but understand the weights of bags from different brands may vary. A small bag may be 3 pounds or 8 pounds. A large bag may be 25 pounds or 40 pounds. This matters when comparing prices.

- Do you have any special needs that must be addressed? Food sensitivities or life stage preferences can narrow your choices fairly quickly. Medical issues may demand a different approach.

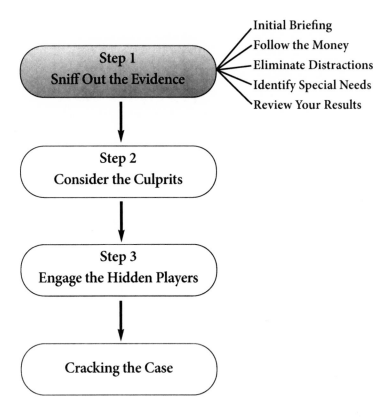

Step 1 has given us a good overview and direction for our investigation. Now let's move on to take a closer look at the evidence we've uncovered and build a case based on facts.

Step 2: Consider the Culprits begins with a glance at the lineup of usual suspects on the Ingredient List. This is where we can sniff out some secrets hiding both on the inside and outside of the dog food package.

Step 2

Consider the Culprits

Spot the Suspects
Interrogate the Ingredients
Expose the Scam of Splitting
Cross Examine Meat, Meal and By-Products

Spot the Suspects:
First Impressions from
the Ingredient List Lineup

Growing up, he was a choirboy.

After initially failing his physical exam for military service, he went on to become a decorated war hero and one of the most visionary leaders of the 20th century. A vegetarian and charismatic speaker, he was fiercely devoted to his country, wife and dog.

Sound like someone you'd like to meet?

First impressions can often be deceiving

Without having more of the story, an early impression can be misleading because it's based on incomplete information. The same holds true when scanning the Ingredient List on a bag of pet food. The Ingredient List often presents a favorable first impression. But we can't just stop there.

How can this be? The Ingredient List tells us what's in the bag. It presents our suspects by name. What else is there to know? Plenty, as it turns out. Accepting the list at face value opens us up to the danger of deception.

Go beyond a first impression to better understand a food

The usual suspects introduced in the Ingredient List tip us off to the quality of a food. These tips include:

1. The form of the primary protein source
2. The amount of an ingredient
3. The form and source of questionable ingredients
4. The number of ingredients listed

We use these tips to determine what to target in a more detailed ingredient interrogation.

Let's look at the various forms a chicken ingredient can take

This popular protein can appear on an Ingredient List as Fresh Chicken, Chicken, Chicken Meal, Chicken by-products, Chicken by-product meal, Poultry, Poultry by-products, Poultry Meal or Poultry by-products meal.

Whew. Can all of this really be chicken? Yep, indeed it can. But wait… there's more!

Each of these forms tells us something about the quality and desirability of the ingredient. We recognize fresh chicken from grocery shopping and it may seem attractive as a pet food ingredient. But as a Dog Food Detective, we look beyond that favorable first impression.

What follows a seemingly attractive ingredient on the list is important because it uncovers critical clues about ingredient weight.

The "weight rule" reveals how much of an ingredient a food contains

The order ingredients appear on the list is not random. By law, the heaviest pet food ingredients must appear first in an Ingredient List. This means that the first few ingredients are the heaviest. They make up the majority of the food *by weight*.

By looking at the first six ingredients, we get a very quick idea of what we'll be feeding. It is in the best interests of manufacturers to make a good first impression with these ingredients. This can often be misleading because of some common tactics used to disguise ingredients.

One ingredient can become many and small amounts of meat can appear at the top of an Ingredient List. Ingredients can easily be manipulated and still comply with the "weight rule."

Just because the heaviest ingredient is listed first, does not mean there's more of it than what follows. Yes, it weighs more, but weight is not the only thing that matters.

Heavier is not always better

It's not uncommon to see a "fresh" meat ingredient, like Fresh Chicken, appear first in an Ingredient List. This is a good start, but can also be deceiving.

Fresh chicken catches our eye when it appears on a bag, and manufacturers use this to their advantage. Remember to go beyond that first impression and look at what comes next.

In the following example, we're off to a great start with Fresh Chicken. A closer look shows that what follows does not offer any more animal protein until we find by-products as the sixth ingredient.

CHICKEN, BREWERS RICE, WHOLE GRAIN WHEAT, CORN GLUTEN MEAL, WHOLE GRAIN CORN, POULTRY BY-PRODUCT MEAL...

Don't be misled when a "fresh" meat appears first in an Ingredient List, but is followed by five non-meat ingredients. Fresh meat is heavy. It can be up to 80% water by weight, which is why it appears early in the list.

What follows a fresh meat ingredient is just as important

Look for at least one other specific meat protein source in the first six ingredients when a fresh meat appears early. This tips us off to what provides most of the food's protein.

That other protein source could be another fresh meat, or a specific meat meal, like Chicken Meal or Lamb Meal. When more meat appears in the first six ingredients, it shows that more protein comes from meat, not other ingredients like grains.

The following example shows another meat protein source following the fresh chicken. We can't always tell if the fresh meat or the meal provides more protein. We can see the protein comes from chicken and not grains.

> CHICKEN, CHICKEN MEAL, OATMEAL,
> BROWN RICE, BARLEY, CHICKEN FAT...

Keep in mind that fresh meat ingredients are heavier than grains or meals. When grains are listed before fresh meats, that shows us the food is primarily cereal. We want to see two or more meat or meat meal ingredients making an appearance in those first six items. If not, take a closer look at exactly what follows the meat ingredient.

A final example leaves no doubt that the protein in this food is coming from meat sources.

> TURKEY, CHICKEN, CHICKEN MEAL, LENTILS,
> YELLOW PEAS, WHITEFISH MEAL, BROWN RICE...

Once our first look has identified the protein form(s) and applied the weight rule, let's scan for more ingredients that may raise red flags.

Proceed cautiously with by-products and preservatives

By-products have a reputation for including some nasty sounding things like heads, feet, and guts. That reputation is a bit dated, and not always accurate, particularly with better quality foods. A first impression shows whether by-products are present. A closer look at the form and source of by-products reveals when they can be considered friend or foe.

A similar caution applies to preservative use. Most pet foods use preservatives to keep fat from going rancid. The two main forms of preservative systems are vitamin-based and chemical-based. The Ingredient List tells us which form is used.

The majority of better quality pet foods now use synthetic vitamin preservative systems. These are primarily vitamins E and C, often listed as Mixed Tocopherols. The chemical preservatives, like BHA, BHT and Ethoxyquin, have proven to be very effective, although questions remain about their safety.

Our initial scan quickly reveals any red flags from by-products and preservatives. A final glimpse at the length of our list rounds out this first impression.

Chuck loved sharing steak dinners with his dog, Bella. When Chuck saw the new Steak & Veggie food on the shelf, he didn't question what was really in the bag before gleefully bringing it home to Bella as a special treat.

It would have only taken a moment to spot Corn and Soybean Meal at the top of the Ingredient List, followed by Meat and Bone Meal. Appearing 9th on the list was a "source of grilled flavor." And Bella's beloved beef? It showed up as the

15th ingredient, just after hydrochloric acid and potassium chloride.

In this case, Chuck's first impression might have alerted him that the Steak & Veggie food was not a suitable substitute for the sirloin that Bella loved so much.

How much good stuff is really in there?

Some foods have a very short Ingredient List. They may contain two or three recognizable ingredients, and a preservative followed by a litany of vitamins and minerals. This approach is often used in limited ingredient diets to address food sensitivities.

Most foods include a dozen or more ingredients, followed by their vitamin/ mineral components. When we see minerals appear with "chelate" following their name, that's a good sign. It indicates the minerals are in a form which is more bio-available to dogs.

Some foods have taken to adding attractive sounding fruits or veggies late in the list. Do all of these ingredients serve a valid nutritional purpose or are they there for show?

Many of these suspects are included simply because they look good to us. Does a dog benefit much from that fruit and veggie blend if it's the 12th listed ingredient just in front of…salt? It's important not to rely solely on a first impression until more questions get answered.

The Ingredient List is a good start but does not tell all

Our first impression comes from a quick glance at the form and source of the first six ingredients on the List, and a scan for red flags.

Early tips that raise red flags can confirm or change our first impression of a food. What appeared attractive initially may now raise more questions. We're finally ready to ask these questions in our Ingredient Interrogation.

Get a better picture of your subject to avoid deception

Remember the former choirboy introduced earlier? Based on the information presented, he likely made a good first impression.

Every bit of the evidence presented about our choirboy is true. It wasn't manipulated, but it also wasn't complete. How accurate was your first impression of Mr. Adolph Hitler based on that biographical glimpse?

Dig a bit beyond the first impression and surprising facts may be uncovered about a food. Let's take a closer look at our initial lineup and begin a brief Ingredient Interrogation.

Captain K says:

"Appearances can be deceiving.

First impressions are fine but don't always tell the whole story.

Questions are key!"

From the "Spotting the Suspects" Evidence Archive:

Deborah had just brought home her first two dogs from the shelter. She had been given some food, but found it too pricey when she went to the pet store for a refill.

She asked about the availability of similar but less expensive options. The clerk produced a food which he claimed was comparable in quality and formula. "It's pretty much the same as what you've been feeding," he said. "The only reason it's cheaper is because this brand doesn't do any advertising."

Deborah brought the new food home and was dismayed to find her new puppies did not like it as much as the original, more expensive food. A few days later, she spotted a bag of dog food on the shelf of her favorite specialty grocery store. "I liked that it had no wheat, was wholesome, and seemed to have a lot of healthy ingredients."

"The dogs love it," she reported. "It is noticeably 'tastier'; I can tell by comparing the old to the new food, without actually tasting it."

This new food did indeed appear to have been made with wholesome ingredients. We'll let the Ingredient List speak for itself:

CHICKEN MEAL, GROUND BROWN RICE, GROUND RICE, GROUND WHOLE WHEAT, CHICKEN FAT, FLAX SEED, HERRING MEAL, TOMATO POMACE, ALFALFA MEAL,

DRIED EGG, NATURAL FLAVORING, BREWERS YEAST, KELP, LECITHIN, SALT, DRIED WHEY, POTASSIUM CHLORIDE, ROSEMARY AND SAGE EXTRACT, VITAMIN/ MINERAL PRE-MIX...

It turns out that Deborah was mistaken: there is wheat in this food. It's just not at the top of the list as it was in the other dog food. Most of these ingredients are recognizable, but there's quite a bit of grain: Ground Brown Rice, Ground Rice, Ground Whole Wheat and Alfalfa Meal. While Herring Meal can be a good source of protein, it appears late in the list, following Flax Seed and Fat.

At first glance, the Ingredient List presents a fairly good picture. But Deborah still needs some more information, despite the favorable first impression.

The big unknowns about the food are its digestibility and how well Debbie's dogs will perform on it. The performance question will be answered over time as the furkids continue to chow down. Some questions about digestibility are answered as we begin our Ingredient Interrogation.

Interrogate the Ingredients:
Deciphering Disguises by Making the Ingredient List Talk

We've plucked our suspects from the lineup and plopped them into the interrogation chair. Any red flags raised by our first impression can now be given the attention they deserve.

A DFD doesn't have to resort to enhanced interrogation methods to extract essential information from ingredient suspects. They are quite cooperative when the proper questions are posed. Ingredients willingly expose valuable information once we understand what's in a name.

There are subtle clues hiding in an ingredient's name

A critical clue contained in an ingredient name is its form. Form shows not only *what* ingredient is used in a food, but how it is used. This helps us better understand an ingredient's true nature.

A closely related clue is the amount, or quantity, of an ingredient used in a food. When we consider ingredient form and quantity together, it puts the Ingredient List into better perspective. Combining these clues reveals the true weight of each ingredient used in a food.

This is particularly important when looking at the first six ingredients of a food. A simple way to put these two clues together is to recognize the difference between whole and processed forms of ingredients.

It's easy to spot the form of an ingredient

Some ingredients are processed whole while others are processed into pieces, or fractions. Whole foods are preferable since they are less processed.

Whole foods are fairly easy to recognize. These ingredients are raised on a farm or grown in a field, with nothing added. Whole food ingredients will appear only once in an Ingredient List. But if a similar name pops up later, that's a fractional ingredient.

Whole food ingredients are good, but they can also be used to present a misleading front for a less than ideal formula. Here's how this can happen.

Whole foods are heavy, and processed foods are light

We know that the first six ingredients of a pet food make up the majority of its weight. When a whole food, like fresh chicken, appears at the top of the list, it's an encouraging sign. When that whole food is followed by even more whole ingredients, all the better.

But it is rare to find a fresh meat ingredient followed by a host of other "good" ingredients. More often than not, fresh meat is followed by processed, fractional ingredients. These ingredients can share a common name, or they can be fractions of different ingredients.

Multiple forms of one ingredient raise a red flag

It is not uncommon to find one ingredient disguised in different forms on an Ingredient List. Each of these forms weighs less than the original, whole ingredient, which affects its position on the Ingredient List.

The list is now misleading because the true nature and amount of the original ingredient in the food is masked. In fact, this is the most common way ingredient weight can be manipulated. We decipher this disguise in more detail in the next chapter on Splitting.

Another cause of confusion with the light and heavy guideline can occur with meat and meal ingredients.

Stephanie thought she was going about her choice in a highly scientific fashion. The label that caught her eye boasted "Real Chicken" as the #1 ingredient and "no Chicken by-product Meal." A quick glance at the start and end of the Ingredient List indeed showed Chicken as the first ingredient with fruits and veggies concluding the list.

Just before placing the bag in the pantry, Stephanie took a closer look at what followed the Fresh Chicken and was shocked at what she saw. Grains, grains and more grains were the primary ingredients of the food she'd just lugged home. A bit of Chicken Meal appeared in the eighth position, too late to be of much consequence. The very end of the list included apples, broccoli, carrots, cranberries and peas.

Now how scientific was that?

Meat vs. meal – who wins?

Most dry pet foods use meal ingredients. Meal is a rendered product, which can use castoffs from the human food industry, quality meats, or both.

So, what is rendering? Rendering is a production process that turns those various meat ingredients into a concentrated source of protein with low moisture and no fat.

There's a healthy debate about the benefits and drawbacks of meal ingredients compared to fresh meat. Both arguments have merit. Some manufacturers insist that their meal ingredients are simply high-quality meat with the moisture removed. Detractors insist that meal ingredients contain lower quality protein that should not be fed. Who's right?

We draw our own conclusions about meat and meal

Meals are only as good as the fresh ingredients used in their production. Using fresh, but poor quality, chicken meat is not necessarily better than using a good quality chicken meal. If the chicken meal is made with good ingredients, it can easily surpass a poor quality fresh meat ingredient.

The quality of both fresh meat and meat meal is determined by the source of the meat. But this information is often hard to uncover. Some manufacturers are quite open and proud of their sources, while others prefer not to reveal this "proprietary information."

When a manufacturer chooses not to talk about its sources, it can indicate that ingredients are chosen based on the lowest cost. These low cost ingredients are commodities, and will vary in consistency and quality. Our cross-examination of meat and meals at the end of this section can help to determine the quality of these foods.

By-products and preservatives also raise questions of quality

By-products and by-product meals are being used in fewer foods these days. This is an encouraging trend since by-products have a rather unsavory history of using discarded scraps from human food production.

By-products can include some good-quality ingredients like kidney, liver and heart. These internal organs can be good sources of nutrition, depending on their origin. By-products can also include heads, feet, intestines, or blood. Unless they are specifically identified by name, we just don't know what we're getting when by-products appear in the Ingredient List.

Most of the better "complete and balanced" foods no longer include by-products unless they specify the form and source. Some excellent products labeled for "intermittent feeding" contain clearly identified internal organs. This is a welcome change from formulas which include questionable "meat or poultry by-products" on their Ingredient Lists.

As with any generic ingredient, if the source is not identified, it's best to steer clear. Given that rule of thumb, a food containing Meat by-product Meal speaks for itself. Combining the unknown generic ingredients of both Meat and By-product Meal raises questions that can't be answered.

Preservative questions are easily answered

Most dry pet foods use preservatives to keep the added fat in the formula from going rancid. Preservatives most often appear in a "chemical" or "vitamin" form.

Chemical preservatives, like BHA, BHT and Ethoxyquin are effective, long-lasting and inexpensive. These are the same preservatives used in human foods, some of which are also found in jet fuel and embalming fluid. Ethoxyquin was originally developed as a pesticide and rubber preservative before being adapted for use as a pet food preservative.

There is a growing perception that these chemical preservatives contribute to cancer. They are easily identified when they appear on the Ingredient List.

Vitamin-based preservatives, usually a synthetic form of Vitamin C or E, are also effective. These laboratory-produced vitamin preservatives are not as long-lasting as their chemical counterparts. Most vitamin-based preservative systems give pet food a shelf life of 12 months or longer.

Pet foods using vitamin preservative systems are often marketed as "naturally preserved." While technically correct, these synthetic vitamin/mineral compounds are not the same as the natural vitamins and minerals found in whole foods.

Some formulas now use sprouted grains or other "live" foods to supply preservative properties, instead of vitamins produced in a laboratory. This is an encouraging, more natural, whole food approach which merits closer scrutiny.

Strip away disguises after an Ingredient Interrogation

Identifying the ingredients in pet food goes beyond what initially meets the eye. When we combine form and quantity of ingredients, we get a much better perspective of a food. Keep the following guidelines in mind when looking at an Ingredient List:

1. Whole ingredients are good, but heavy
2. Repetitive listing of one ingredient in different forms can be deceptive
3. Specific meat or meal is better than generic meat or meal
4. Chemical preservative systems are used by lower quality foods

These guidelines help identify the true nature of a food.

Let's look a little closer now at that second guideline, and see how the deception of splitting ingredients can be shattered by a Dog Food Detective.

Captain K says:

"Good Ingredients, like good friends, can be hard to find.
Now we know how to look.
Hang out with your true buddies, and kick those posers
to the curb!"

From the "Ingredient Interrogation" Evidence Archive:

Dog food formulas are constantly changing. Companies are sold and new formulas appear. What is in fashion today may become "new and improved" tomorrow. When that happens, it's to our benefit to determine whether we agree with the definition of "improved."

Ingredient definitions can change and new forms of protein may appear. Reformulations are common and often go unannounced and unnoticed. Some changes improve a formula, others improve a company's bottom line.

One topic currently under discussion is whether "pulse" or "feather meal" should be used as a source of protein. Pulse, more commonly known as peas, can be used as a protein, starch, fiber or flour depending on how it is processed.

Feathers have a high protein content, but are undigestible unless processed. Since all kibble uses processed ingredients, it's quite possible Feather Meal or Pulse Protein will land in the first six ingredients of a new formula some day soon.

Here's how the first five ingredients of one major pet food has changed over the years:

1984: MEAT MEAL, GROUND YELLOW CORN, ANIMAL FAT, BEET PULP, BREWER'S YEAST

1987: GROUND CORN, MEAT MEAL, POULTRY BY-PRODUCT MEAL, ANIMAL FAT, BEET PULP

1990: GROUND CORN, POULTRY BY-PRODUCT MEAL, MEAT MEAL, ANIMAL FAT, BEET PULP

1991: CHICKEN BY-PRODUCT MEAL, GROUND CORN, RICE FLOUR, ANIMAL FAT, BEET PULP

1998: CHICKEN BY-PRODUCT MEAL, GROUND CORN, RICE FLOUR, GROUND GRAIN SORGHUM, ANIMAL FAT

2008: CHICKEN, CORN MEAL, GROUND WHOLE GRAIN SORGHUM, CHICKEN BY-PRODUCT MEAL, CHICKEN FAT, DRIED BEET PULP

2010: CHICKEN, CORN MEAL, GROUND WHOLE GRAIN SORGHUM, CHICKEN BY-PRODUCT MEAL, DRIED BEET PULP, CHICKEN FLAVOR

2011-2013: CHICKEN, CORN MEAL, GROUND WHOLE GRAIN SORGHUM, CHICKEN BY-PRODUCT MEAL, DRIED BEET PULP, CHICKEN FLAVOR, CHICKEN FAT

So what is the lesson here, besides an ever-changing formula?

Chances are, most pet parents who fed this food over the years had no idea of the changes in formulation. It appears that most of these changes were for the better. Animal Fat made way for Chicken Fat. Meat Meal became Chicken by-product Meal, which then became Chicken.

Another noticeable change over the years has been the increasing quantity of grains. "Fresh" chicken appeared in 2008, along with concentrated Corn Meal which replaced Ground Corn. Chicken by-product Meal moved from first to fourth on the list, and Rice Flour disappeared.

What does this tell us? The primary protein source (Chicken by-product Meal) was replaced with a fresh ingredient which can be 70% water. There's more grain by weight from both Corn Meal and Sorghum than from the next meat protein source (Chicken by-product Meal).

A "fresh" chicken ingredient followed by multiple grain ingredients can raise questions about the quality and quantity of protein coming from animal sources.

We'll now take a closer look at why this question arises as we examine a common practice known as splitting.

Expose the Scam of Splitting:
How to Recognize Ingredient Identity Theft

Ever bite into a beautiful apple only to spit it out in disgust?

What appears as a perfectly ripe, juicy treat suddenly turns into mealy mush in your mouth. Sure, it's still an apple, but it was carefully created for appearance, rather than taste or nutrition.

The packaging is lovely, but it hides what is truly inside.

Splitting hides the truth about pet food ingredients

Splitting is a routine practice which breaks an ingredient into smaller, lighter parts. It is the most common way to mask the true nature and amount of an ingredient in a pet food.

When the name of an ingredient appears in more than one form, that's called splitting. Each of the forms is a part, or *fraction*, of the original whole ingredient.

For example, when Whole Brown Rice is split, it can appear as Rice, Rice Bran, Rice Flour, White Rice, Brewer's Rice and more.

At first glance, this seems fine. But let's look past that first impression to see through this common scheme.

Splitting allows Ingredient Lists to be developed for appearance

When an ingredient is split into fractional parts, each of those parts weighs less than the original ingredient. For example, take a cup of brown rice that weighs 6 ounces. Now, split that cup of rice into three separate ingredients: flour, white rice, and rice bran.

What started out as 6 ounces of brown rice is now 2 ounces of flour, 3 ounces of white rice and 1 ounce of rice bran. But why do we care?

The law requires ingredients to be listed in order of their weight.

Since each individual component is lighter than the original whole ingredient, they can now appear further down in the ingredient listing. As those fractions move further down in the listing, heavier items, like Chicken, can move up.

Reducing ingredient weight moves it lower on the list

We've learned that the first six ingredients are most critical and make up the majority of our pet food by weight. *Splitting drops the position of lower quality or less desirable ingredients by reducing their individual weights.*

Just because those split ingredients appear lower on the list does not mean a food contains less of them. Splitting only makes a food appear more attractive. What is truly a Rice and Chicken food can now legally be called Chicken and Rice.

Dog Food Detectives are never fooled by this ploy. Simply scanning a bit further down the Ingredient List can reveal fractioned ingredients. This clue can always expose a lower quality food.

Here's how splitting makes a food attractive

Let's consider the Ingredient List of a pet food containing 3 ounces of Chicken and 6 ounces of Brown Rice. We've learned that ingredients must be listed in order by weight, so this food would list Brown Rice before Chicken.

Many pet parents seek out foods which list meat as the first ingredient. So our example pet food, with Brown Rice as its first ingredient, isn't desirable from a marketing perspective.

Splitting allows Chicken to be nudged to the first spot on the Ingredient List. Split the Brown Rice into fractions and suddenly those 3 ounces of Chicken weigh more than any of the individual rice fractions. Perfect! Chicken can now be listed first just like this:

> CHICKEN, WHOLE BROWN **RICE**, GROUND
> WHOLE WHITE **RICE**, **RICE** BRAN, BREWERS **RICE**,
> **RICE** HULLS, ETC

The same type of trickiness plays out when two or more ingredient are split:

> CHICKEN, SOYBEAN MEAL, SOY FLOUR, ANIMAL
> FAT, BREWERS RICE, SOY PROTEIN CONCENTRATE,
> CORN GLUTEN MEAL, GROUND YELLOW CORN

While this food has less rice than our previous example, the combination of soy, corn and rice still outweigh the chicken ingredient.

CAPTAIN K'S
Case File

Ellen walked into the big pet shop and was immediately attracted to a shiny new display of food.

"This is our newest line," the clerk said proudly. "It's made with fresh chicken and has no chicken meal or by-products. You won't find anything else like it in the store!"

Ellen took a quick look at the label and frowned. "It doesn't seem to have much meat in it at all," she said.

The clerk look puzzled and pointed at the bag. "Sure it does. See, chicken is the first ingredient and then there's just some soy and rice. It's mostly chicken- it says so right on the label!"

A closer look at the first six ingredients revealed three different soy fractions, mingled among rice and corn parts. Ellen tried to explain this to the clerk, but he had only been instructed to point out the first ingredient and the absence of chicken meal and by-products.

We want more meat than that other stuff!

An understanding of splitting trains us to regularly check for ingredients which are split into component parts. In the previous example, it's easy to spot the splitting of both soy and corn.

When a meat ingredient is followed by a litany of unrelated fractions, that's a dead giveaway of a lower-quality formulation.

Whole Brown Rice is a decent ingredient. Rice Bran and Brewers Rice are poor substitutes. Ground Yellow Corn can be a reasonable addition to a food while Corn Hulls, or Corn Grits really don't add much to the quality. The same holds true for fractioned ingredients like Oat Bran, Wheat Middlings, Corn Gluten and other unrecognizables.

When you see a meat ingredient leading the Ingredient List, pay close attention to what follows. If the meat is followed by fractioned ingredients and nothing else, you've just identified a splitting scam.

What about multiple meat ingredients?

It's not unusual to see meat ingredients appear multiple times in a list. This can be an example of where splitting may work to our advantage. Fresh Chicken, Chicken Meal, Chicken by-products, and Chicken by-product Meal are the most common forms of meat ingredients.

As long as the protein source is named (beef, lamb, duck, turkey, etc.), we're on the right track. When the protein source is generic, like "meat" or "poultry," it immediately raises a red flag. These generic proteins are found in lower quality foods.

A food may list a specific protein source in both a fresh and a meal form. Remember that fresh meat contains a huge amount of water. The weight of the water can often push a fresh meat ingredient to the top of an ingredient list. Don't be fooled by that first heavy, watery ingredient.

Look for whole, not split, ingredients following a fresh meat. If there is an additional named meat protein in the first six ingredients, all the better. Any additional meat protein should be from a specific species (chicken, lamb, salmon) rather than a generic source (poultry, meat, fish). Additional named meat protein sources tell us the food has a decent amount of animal protein.

Splitting is easily recognized

It becomes routine to spot splitting and its tricky effects as we scan the Ingredient List on a pet food bag. A sure giveaway is the appearance of multiple forms of a single ingredient early in the list. Just being aware of the practice helps us avoid the deception of splitting scams. It's an essential step in recognizing what truly makes up our pet food.

By shining the light of understanding on fractional ingredients and their positions on the Ingredient List, this part of our detective work becomes second nature.

Let's build on this step as we dig a bit deeper into unmasking some other common cons hiding in, and on, your pet food bag. A closer look at the Meat vs. Meal debate shows how it can also lead to misunderstanding.

Captain K says:
"Splitting is an easy scam to bust.
We want the whole ingredient, not bits and pieces.
How many times do you want to pay for the same thing
called by a different name?"

From the "Splitting" Evidence Archives:

In the previous Case File, a misinformed clerk tried to steer Ellen towards a popular Chicken flavored dog food.

To the clerk's credit, the food did indeed use Chicken as its first ingredient. While the Ingredient List of this food could certainly be worse, it's not particularly attractive when we examine it using what we've learned so far.

To give this food the benefit of the doubt, let's go well beyond the first six ingredients:

CHICKEN, SOYBEAN MEAL, SOY FLOUR, ANIMAL FAT
PRESERVED WITH MIXED-TOCOPHEROLS (FORM OF
VITAMIN E), BREWERS RICE, SOY PROTEIN CONCENTRATE,
CORN GLUTEN MEAL, GROUND YELLOW CORN, GLYCERIN,
GROUND WHEAT, POULTRY BY-PRODUCT MEAL, ANIMAL
DIGEST, OAT MEAL...

Here's what Captain K has to say about this suspect...

- the first ingredient is fresh chicken, which is mostly water by weight
- the primary protein may not come from meat
- no other animal protein ingredient is listed until poultry by-product meal at #11
- too much soy and corn, both in fractioned forms
- red flags from splitting, generic animal fat, very little animal protein

Get the picture?

Even though fresh chicken appears at the top of the list, a heavier meal ingredient (soybean meal) follows immediately after. This concentrated meal ingredient is a non-meat protein source.

The combined weight of the fractioned grain ingredients (soy and corn) most likely outweigh the meat. Meat should provide the primary protein and nutrients of a formula. In this food, the primary nutrition comes from soy, unspecified by-products and corn.

More than likely, the majority of this food's protein comes from Soybean Meal rather than fresh Chicken.

Now let's take a look at some facts and fiction about Meat and Meal.

Cross-Examine Meat, Meal and By-Products:
Confusing Confessions From Two Rival Families

Once we begin to see through the scam of splitting, our investigation becomes much simpler. Split ingredients are revealed with just a glance. Now we're ready to coax a confession from two other important ingredient families: meats and by-products.

By-products are usually an open and shut case. But different tactics are required to get meats to confess. While closely related, meats and meat meals pose a bit of a dilemma.

There's a rivalry between meat and meal that needs closer examination. Sometimes these two suspects don't offer much information. Questioning their background helps us to avoid mystery and misunderstanding.

Incomplete information leads to confusion

There is a growing contingent of advocates who maintain that fresh meat ingredients are superior to meals. This is a valid argument, although it can also come from a position of ignorance. Pet food ingredients have a very specific definition of what can be considered "Fresh."

CAPTAIN K'S
Case File

AAFCO defines "Fresh" as "ingredient(s) having not been subject to freezing, to treatment by cooking, drying, rendering, hydrolysis, or similar process, or the addition of salt, curing agents, natural or synthetic chemical preservatives or other processing aids, or to preservation by means other than refrigeration."

Fresh meat, for purposes of pet food, can be pretty much what you'd expect...except when it is not. And therein lies the mystery. To simplify our understanding, let's get more specific and confine our investigation to some of the mysteries of chicken.

Chicken is one of the most common pet food ingredients

It appears as Fresh Chicken, Chicken, Chicken Meal, Chicken by-products and Poultry in its various forms. We'll save Poultry for last, since that brings us full circle with a generic description, like Meat.

The highest quality chicken ingredient starts with clean muscle meat. This certainly meets the AAFCO definition of "Fresh Chicken," but is rarely the only chicken we find in a pet food.

Chicken in pet food can also include skin, bone, and some organ meats. It can come in a variety of forms and quality, just like what's found in the meat case of your grocery store.

For example, a whole chicken, a package of wings, or a boneless breast all meet the definition of "Fresh" if not previously frozen or injected with preservatives. Locally grown, free range, with giblets, backs, breasts, necks, skinless, boneless, and southern grown are additional options. And don't forget those discounted, soon-to-expire, semi-rancid packages oozing juices in the corner.

But when shopping for dog food, we're not able to browse the meat case and choose our chicken. So how do we know which chicken ingredient we're getting? We don't. But at least we do know we're getting chicken "suitable for use in animal food."

What is suitable for use in animal food?

How does chicken fit for human consumption compare with chicken suitable for use in animal food? All chicken in the grocery store has been USDA inspected and certified as human edible. All chicken ingredients in pet food are not.

Some pet food companies have faced legal trouble for making claims that their food used "human grade ingredients." That term may seem like a clear description to us but was considered misleading by the court. Unless every ingredient in a pet food is human edible, the term "human grade" cannot be used. Fines were paid and labels were changed. The regulations prevailed.

Yet these same regulations still allow for some pretty nasty things to be used in animal food. The standards of quality for pet food are certainly lower than what we think of as "human grade."

While most reputable manufacturers avoid the lower-end ingredients, there is no law against using 4-D meats (dead, dying, diseased, disabled). It's also not uncommon for chicken ingredients to come from USDA inspected, human food production plants. When chicken from those plants doesn't pass a USDA inspection, that meat can still be used in pet food.

A company can claim its ingredients are USDA inspected

Ingredients may indeed be produced in a plant that is USDA inspected. The ingredients may even include meats that have been inspected. But inspections can sometimes uncover problems.

USDA inspections often find ingredients that are not up to human standards. When this occurs, these ingredients may become… "suitable for use in animal food."

Hmmmm.

While this can raise more questions than it answers, it's an important point to keep in mind. The quality of chicken, or any meat, as an ingredient can range from poor to excellent. We can't know for certain without contacting the company or touring the manufacturing plant.

The same is true for chicken meal

Chicken meal can begin with chicken in any form or level of quality. The chicken is then cooked or *rendered*. Rendering is the not so simple process of using heat, pressure and steam to produce a concentrated protein source.

During the rendering process chicken becomes… mush. The mush is then processed to remove fat and reduce the moisture content to 10% or less. Voila– Chicken Meal!

Chicken Meal is a concentrated ingredient with about three times the protein of fresh chicken and no fat. Since most of the moisture has been removed, meal ingredients are much lighter than fresh meat ingredients.

It's a bit like reducing a cup of whole milk to a spoonful of powdered milk. Or a jug of fresh squeezed orange juice to concentrate. All the benefits of the original ingredient at a fraction of the weight. Just add water.

The argument in the store was getting heated before it took a turn towards the ridiculous. "You don't know what you're talking about," shouted Anne. "I've seen the YouTube videos of how they make pet food. They just dump that slurry of dead animal parts out of the cooker for more processing."

Deb came over and calmly put an arm around her shoulder. "I'm sure you're right about that, Anne," she said reassuringly. "But it's a link in the recycling chain. After all, we use and eat rendered products every day. When was the last time you enjoyed some gravy, jello or washed with soap? All those products use rendered ingredients, too."

Anne and Deb represent opposite viewpoints. Anne wants nothing to do with rendered ingredients because she's convinced they're all roadkill. But Deb sees no problem in using an economical source of protein that would otherwise be wasted. Both viewpoints have merit, depending on your personal preferences.

Does this mean Chicken Meal is better than Fresh Chicken?

The same questions of quality apply to both Chicken and Chicken Meal. The quality of the chicken meat used to make meal offers the best clues about the quality of the meal produced. Chicken meal made with free range or organic chicken will certainly be superior to fresh chicken from factory farms.

If we start with sour milk or tasteless oranges, the inferior quality shows up in the concentrate they produce. If we start with poor quality chicken, we'll end up with poor quality chicken meal.

As a rendered product, we can be certain that chicken meal is much higher in protein than the same weight of fresh chicken. Beyond that, it's anyone's guess. The rendering process is the main reason there's such an ongoing rivalry between the two ingredient families. Rendering is also a source of confusion with meat's sometimes sinister sibling, by-products.

Rendering and by-products: guilt by association

Rendering is a term often used interchangeably with by-products, which is misleading. While most by-products in pet food are rendered, not all rendered ingredients are by-products.

By-products include many of the "cast off" pieces of an animal that are not normally found in higher-quality human foods. We find by-products in luncheon meats, hot dogs, sausage and many fast food meats. Gelatin is also considered a by-product. But not all by-products are cast offs.

Even though classified as by-products, identified organ meats, like liver, heart and kidney, can be excellent ingredients. Like any meat ingredient, the source of these organ meats determines their quality.

It's rare to see pet food by-products identified beyond their originating source. They most commonly appear as "chicken by-products" or "chicken by-product meal."

It's best to avoid by-products and by-product meals unless they answer questions by specifying their sources. When the generic ingredients Meat or Meat Meal appear, our questions are answered. These generic animal proteins are typically found only in lower quality foods.

Generic Ingredients Defy Description

When we see Chicken Meal listed as an ingredient, we have a sense of what we're getting. When we see Meat Meal listed, we haven't got a clue. Meat Meal can contain just about any type of meat. It's considered a generic ingredient since it is not associated with a specific animal source.

What goes into Meat Meal? Just about any type of meat imaginable. Bison, horse, zoo animals, and/ or beef parts can all be included. 4-D meat (dead, dying, diseased or downer animals) could also be components of Meat Meal or Meat by-product Meal.

Consistency is not a standard for meat ingredients

One batch of Meat Meal may contain radically different elements from the next. Since we can't be certain about what we're getting in a Meat Meal ingredient, it's best to steer clear.

Poultry is the fowl equivalent of the "Meat" ingredient. Poultry can come from chicken, turkey, duck or other birds. Like "Meat," we just don't know what we're getting. It's the same with poultry by-products. Another mystery.

"Meat" and "Poultry" ingredients are inexpensive, unknown sources of protein. We're much better off choosing foods that clearly identify their protein sources. This allows us to better understand and control what's being fed.

When a food uses generic ingredients, like Meat or Poultry as a protein source, it's a clear indication of poor quality.

Solving the mystery of meats

You and I would certainly prefer to sit down to a plate of freshly cooked chicken rather than a pile of powder. But given what happens to that fresh chicken as it's transformed into kibble, our dogs don't have the same choice. When looking at meats vs. meals, an element of mystery remains.

Fortunately, we have a helpful tipster that can help solve the mystery. This informant provides our next source of evidence. It can be found in an often overlooked and underutilized resource known as the Feeding Guidelines.

Captain K says:

"*Coq au vin or KFC?*

The difference is in the preparation and the source.

And then of course, there's the sauce.

No wonder there's a difference in price!"

From the "4-D Meat Discussion" Evidence Archive:

(The following conversation was not admitted into evidence. It was struck from the record but is considered important background information.)

Cornelia was concerned about some things she had heard about the way pet food was made. "I've seen videos showing how some manufacturers use dead pets and other really awful stuff in their foods. How can I spot and avoid this? Seems like that's more important than worrying about grains or chicken protein."

"This is an important point to address," agreed Captain K. "I share your concern, although it's an issue that can introduce an unnecessary level of fear into choosing a dog food. Some of the books and internet articles describing unsavory manufacturing practices present an incomplete picture and offer no solution. If your choice is to feed kibble, you want a reliable way to ensure that what you buy avoids these nasty ingredients.

"The truly awful stuff is out there—less than it used to be—but it is still out there. It's mainly found in grocery and warehouse stores these days. Fortunately, the DFD System helps you eliminate those suspects from consideration.

"Now, I can't say this with 100% certainly, but I do believe that any of the foods that stand up to our System won't be using 4-D meats. The only way to know for certain is to track each batch of ingredients back to their originating source. That's just not practical for a consumer.

"The most reliable way to avoid the problem is to make your own food or feed raw. But that's not a realistic option for most of us. If that does become our choice, we have an entirely different level of control over pet food ingredients.

"Some pet parents say they want to avoid all possibility of 4-D meat, but can't fathom the idea of preparing their own food. Or feeding raw. Or even using a dehydrated mix because of its cost. What they say, and what they're willing to do, and accept, can be quite different. In the end, frustration triumphs and they go back to feeding what's comfortable because they feel helpless. However, the DFD System can change those feelings of frustration.

"The System eliminates 99.9% of the chances that the truly awful stuff will be an issue when making a purchasing decision. We don't have to look for the 4-D ingredients themselves. It's simpler to look at clues which reduce the possibility that low quality ingredients are used in a food."

The System helps us do just that, instead of becoming distracted by a path of investigation that leads in directions we cannot realistically follow.

Informants also play a key role in helping to eliminate these distractions as well. Let's do a quick review before moving on to meet one of our trusted informants.

Summary: Step 2
Consider the Culprits

- Form your first impression of a food by scanning the first six ingredients.

- Go beyond the first impression by looking at the form and position of the primary protein source. Then scan for red flags.

- Red flags include ingredient splitting, chemical preservatives, and generic ingredients.

- Non-meat ingredients following a fresh meat at the beginning of the list is worth a closer look.

- Pay attention to the form of an ingredient and whether by-products are identified or generic.

- Make certain enough protein is coming from meat sources, especially when a fresh meat is listed first.

- The quality of both meat and meals is determined by the quality of the source ingredients. Poor quality chicken makes poor quality chicken meal.

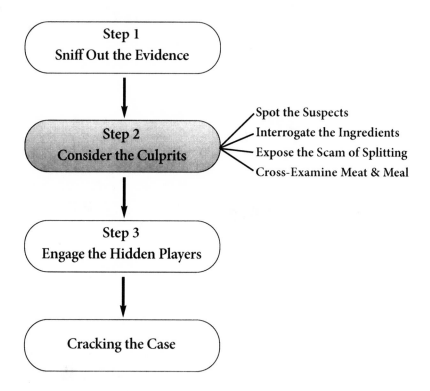

Now that we have a better sense of our suspects, we're ready to move on to Step 3: Engage the Hidden Players.

To find out what may be hiding in the shadows, let's begin with a visit to a trusted informant: the Feeding Guidelines.

Step 3

Engage the Hidden Players

Employ the Informant
Review the Forensics of Guaranteed Analysis
Recognize Tips, Tricks and Traps of Labels

Employ the Informant:
How Feeding Guidelines Offer Tips to Pet Food Value

To the untrained eye, it was a simple chalk mark on a mailbox. Thousands of people walked by it each day without a second glance. An enlightened few understood its importance.

This seemingly insignificant public scribble was a critical piece of evidence which led to the arrest of CIA agent Aldrich Ames. For more than 10 years, Ames had been passing state secrets to the Soviets. The mailbox markings were used to signal clandestine meetings.

Trained observers recognized those easily overlooked marks as something far more important than random squiggles to be ignored.

Feeding Guidelines serve as mailbox chalk marks

Found on every bag of dog food, Feeding Guidelines reveal critical information in an often overlooked form. Their tips help to reveal a dog food's quality and value.

Feeding Guidelines are usually based on a dog's age, weight and activity level. They are the manufacturer's recommendation of how much food should be fed each day to meet minimum nutritional levels.

These minimum nutritional levels are set to ensure our pets receive adequate daily nourishment. Much like the minimum daily requirement numbers appearing on human food packaging, the nutritional guidelines for dogs are standardized.

These standards help us compare the quality of foods when Ingredient Lists appear similar. A difference in Feeding Guidelines provides a critical clue in our investigation.

Feeding Guidelines are one of the few standards for comparison among pet foods

Feeding Guidelines appear on every bag or can of pet food that is considered "nutritionally complete." The differences in these guidelines result from the wide variety of ingredients and quality of our pet foods.

Feeding Guidelines are determined by pet food manufacturers in one of two ways. The most accurate guidelines are developed using feeding trials. Guidelines can also be determined by laboratory analysis. Although feeding trials may more accurately reflect real life experience, both methods reflect the nutritional analysis of a food.

A food meets its "nutritional targets" when its analysis reflects adequate levels of protein, fat, vitamins, minerals, and other nutrients. Both high and low quality food can meet these targets. *The difference in quality can be reflected in how much of a particular food is needed to reach them.* This is where the Feeding Guidelines act as our informant.

High-quality ingredients make a more digestible food

When comparing similar ingredient labels, it's the Feeding Guidelines that tip us off to digestibility. Lower Feeding Guideline numbers equal higher digestibility. Higher digestibility equals higher-quality food.

Digestibility is an important indicator of ingredient and food quality. Digestibility is simply the process of breaking food down to provide nutrients and energy. With a highly-digestible food, more nutrients are available from smaller amounts of food.

A dog uses less energy to process and extract nutrients from a highly-digestible formula. This leaves more energy for normal activities, including play. Since daily nutrients are available from smaller meals, weight is easier to control.

An additional benefit from smaller meals appears after feeding. Since these foods are digested more fully, there is less waste to clean up!

Does feeding less lead to hungry pets?

A highly-digestible pet food will satisfy most dogs. It can be difficult to accept that just 2 cups per day is sufficient for a 50-pound dog if we're accustomed to pouring twice that amount into a bowl. Just keep in mind that the digestibility of the new food is greater, so less is needed to meet the nutritional requirements each day.

When switching from one food to another, it's essential to compare Feeding Guidelines. Because of differences in digestibility, better-quality foods are generally fed in smaller daily servings than lower-quality foods. Without comparing the Feeding Guidelines, it's easy to overfeed. If the serving size is not reduced, the pounds may begin to pile on within just a few days.

We may also save money when comparing Feeding Guidelines of different foods.

Lower feeding guidelines can mean lower food costs

A bag of highly-digestible food lasts longer than a lower-quality food. Why? Because we feed less of that highly- digestible food each day. This saves money since the food bag is replaced less frequently.

We may spend more for a bag of higher-quality food. But we feed less, so our daily feeding cost is reduced. The bag lasts longer, which saves money over time. The proof is in the numbers.

Lisa was dismayed to find her $40 bag of food missing from the shelf. She asked at the counter about a suitable replacement and balked at the price of the suggestion. It would stretch her budget quite a bit. Wasn't there anything less expensive?

There absolutely was. A cheaper food would be a much better choice for the shop. But not for Lisa.

She could choose a different $40 food and return in under 3 weeks for a refill. Or she could pony up the extra $20 and not return for another month. It was a classic "pay me now or pay me later" moment.

Lisa gladly chose the more expensive bag, knowing she had just saved herself some money by reading her mailbox chalk marks found in the Feeding Guidelines.

It's easy to determine the true feeding cost of a food

Simply divide the price of a bag by the number of days it lasts to find the daily cost. The number of days it lasts is determined by how much is fed each day. The amount fed each day is determined by... you guessed it... the Feeding Guidelines.

You may be surprised to find that a $40 bag of food is actually more expensive to feed than a $60 bag of food. The math doesn't lie. The Feeding Guidelines keep the numbers honest.

Feeding Guidelines are informative but not infallible

Whether they've been calculated in a lab or by feeding trials, Feeding Guidelines offer us excellent clues. They provide a good standard of comparison between foods but are recommendations, not gospel.

Adjustments may be needed depending on how a particular dog performs when fed according to the guidelines. Some dogs may require more of a particular food to maintain weight, and others less. The guidelines provide an ideal place to begin, but should not be blindly accepted as gospel.

Its easy to overlook what's in plain sight

Feeding Guidelines are often overlooked when comparing foods. When we know how to recognize what they represent, they are an excellent indication of digestibility, quality and value.

Far from being hidden, they appear on every bag, just waiting to be discovered. They are one of our best informants and should be used by every alert Dog Food Detective. The secrets uncovered in Ingredient Interrogations and Feeding Guidelines are the heart of the Dog Food Detective System.

A more familiar informant, the Guaranteed Analysis, also appears on every package. Now let's see why this character should be viewed with much more skepticism than Feeding Guidelines.

Captain K says:

"Digestibility of a food is an excellent indiction of quality.
Feeding Guidelines are your helpful informant.
Just remember that less is more."

From the "Informants" Evidence Archive:

To make the case for Feeding Guidelines and digestibility more understandable, let's look at two foods with similar Ingredient Lists, but different Feeding Guidelines.

Food #1:
Ingredients: CHICKEN, CHICKEN MEAL, WHOLE BROWN RICE, BREWERS RICE, RICE BRAN, WHOLE GRAIN OATMEAL...
Feeding Guideline for 45-pound Dog: 3.25 cups
Cost of 30 lb bag: $59.99

Food # 2:
Ingredients: CHICKEN MEAL, GROUND BROWN RICE, RICE BRAN, CHICKEN FAT, GROUND OATS, BEET PULP...
Feeding Guideline for 50-pound dog: 2 cups
Cost of 30 lb bag: $63.99

In this example we see two chicken-based formulas which both use rice and oats. Food #1 looks good with two meat protein sources. But it requires almost half again as much volume to be fed based on the feeding guidelines-3.25 cups vs. 2 cups.

This example is all the more obvious when we notice the Feeding Guideline for Food #1 is listed for a 45-pound dog rather than a 50-pound dog. A 50-pound dog would require slightly more food than is recommended.

Some simple math reveals just how much of a difference these Feeding Guidelines make to our pocketbook.

The bag of Food #1 will be emptied much sooner than Food #2. For every 3 bags of Food #1 purchased, only 2 bags of Food #2 will be bought. The next step is a cost comparison over time to determine the true feeding cost.

Let's be generous and round the guideline for Food #1 down to an even 3 cups. We'll use a convenient "Rule of Paw" to say that there are 3 cups/ pound. This means a 30 lb bag contains 90 cups of food (3 cups X 30 lb= 90 cups).

Food #1
Cups fed per day: 3
# of cups in 30 lb bag: 90
# of days bag will last: 30 (number of cups in bag divided by number of cups fed per day)
Cost of food bag: $59.99
Cost to feed per day: $2.00 (cost of food bag divided by number of days the bag lasts)
Monthly cost: $60.00 (daily cost X 30 days)
Annual cost: $730.00 (daily cost X 365 days)

Food #2
Cups fed per day: 2
# of cups in 30 lb bag: 90
# of days bag will last: 45 (number of cups in bag divided by number of cups fed per day)
Cost of food bag: $63.99
Cost to feed per day: $1.42 (cost of food bag divided by number of days the bag lasts)
Monthly cost: $42.60 (daily cost X 30 days)
Annual cost: $518.30 (daily cost X 365 days)

The numbers speak for themselves. Spending a bit more for Food #2 with better Feeding Guidelines saves over $200/year.

Looking at food costs over a year reinforces the value of Feeding Guidelines. They are a trustworthy tool to use for both quality and cost comparisons.

Another informant, the Guaranteed Analysis, should not be trusted in the same way. Let's learn more about the uncertainty behind Guaranteed Analysis numbers as we look closer at this popular informant.

Review the Forensics of "Guaranteed Analysis"

Every good detective knows a case can't be built on a faulty foundation.

A faulty foundation results in questionable conclusions, even with pet foods. Human foods use the Nutrition Facts panel to provide nutrient comparisons. Pet foods have Feeding Guidelines and the Guaranteed Analysis panel. The Guaranteed Analysis lists the percentage of protein, fat, fiber and moisture in a pet food.

These numbers appear on all pet food packaging and are required by law. Guaranteed Analysis (GA) reflects a range of numbers that are frequently used to compare one food against another. Many pet parents rely on Guaranteed Analysis numbers to help choose or evaluate a pet food.

Looking for a high Protein food? Comparing GA numbers reveals which food has the higher percentage of Protein. But how useful are these numbers?

The GA numbers on pet foods are often misunderstood

While all pet foods list Guaranteed Analysis on their labels, the meaning of these numbers are not what we might expect. Using GA numbers to compare the Protein content of one dry food against another is thought to offer an accurate comparison.

On the surface, it does. And since we have no other readily available information to make these types of comparisons, we'll just have to take the GA numbers at face value. In these cases of "apples to apples" comparisons, it's the best we've got. But what are those numbers truly telling us about our nutrients? Not quite as much as first meets the eye.

These numbers need some refining

Do Guaranteed Analysis numbers really tell us how much Protein, Fat, Fiber and Moisture are in our pet's food? It says so right on the label. But let's look beyond the numbers on the label.

Those familiar GA numbers and nutrients appear as Crude listings. Similar to crude oil that must be refined prior to becoming useful as fuel, these numbers do not represent "useable" nutrients.

During the refining process, more than half the volume of crude oil is wasted or extracted for other uses. We start with a gallon of crude oil, and end up with less than a half gallon of useable fuel after refining.

Our dog's metabolism is the equivalent of the refinery

When we see Crude Protein listed as a percentage in the GA, that's not what our dog receives as useable, or digestible, protein. It's merely the starting point of what is broken down into useable nutrients and waste.

The GA numbers do us the favor of identifying themselves as Crude. But they do not tell us how much is actually useable. We're far more interested in what's actually digested and available for our pet.

That's where those GA numbers begin to get interesting ... and mysteriously misleading.

"I remember seeing a spiffy looking brochure back in the 1990s that was briefly promoted by a major pet food company. It featured a pair of old boots, some motor oil, and wood scraps. A test 'food' made from these ingredients exceeded the recommended Protein, Fat and Fiber levels set by AAFCO.

The company was promoting the fact that their food used superior ingredients, unlike their competitors. Their message was to trust the ingredients, not the numbers. There was a certain irony to this, since their ingredients weren't all that great. But they were certainly better than those used in the test food!"

Don't compare apples to oranges

When we compare Crude Protein to Crude Protein, that's a fair comparison. But somewhere along the way, pet parents began to use GA numbers to help determine which pet food was "better" than another. GA became a measure of quality. If a food had a higher Protein content, it was "better." If it had lower Fiber, it was "better."

Using GA numbers to determine quality is not useful because too much information is missing. It's like comparing apples to oranges and doesn't give us an accurate comparison of quality.

GA numbers tell us nothing about the quality of a food

While useful in direct comparisons, GA numbers don't give us an accurate accounting of what many have come to expect.

When we look at the components of the GA, we expect to learn the actual percentage of Protein, Fat, Fiber and Moisture. Sadly, that is not the case.

The Fat content? Yes, it could be 14% as listed on the label. But legally, it could just as likely be 18%. And of that 18%, it's very possible that half of it is unusable, or wasted.

How can this be?

The GA uses a range of values which add uncertainty

Rather than using exact numbers, the GA appears as a minimum or maximum range of values. Along with the uncertainty of the Crude form of nutrients, these ranges throw us further off track.

Even if we could determine how much of a food's Crude component were useable, the GA still leaves us hanging on this other critical detail: we don't truly know how much of that nutrient is in the bag.

Take another look at those GA numbers and notice that in addition to the Crude terminology, we see the words *Minimum* and *Maximum*. What the heck does that mean?

Simply stated, the Protein and Fat content reflected in the GA will be *no less* than the percentage shown. It's the opposite for Fiber and Moisture, because they reflect Maximum levels. These will be at a level that does not *exceed* what appears on the label.

Just like the Crude numbers, these minimum and maximum ranges hint at what may be in the bag. AAFCO regulations prohibit the range from being displayed as a sliding scale (18-22%), which could offer slightly more guidance. The crude range just doesn't provide solid evidence of what is truly there.

Why pay attention to Guaranteed Analysis at all?

The intent behind listing the GA on pet food is to ensure adequate levels of nutrients in a food. These levels, like our human Nutrition Facts, represent minimum required nutrient levels for our pets.

GA numbers work as a standard for comparing foods when those are the only numbers being compared. They tell us nothing about quality, digestibility or actual nutritional content of a food.

There are other more important and useful factors to consider rather than relying solely on GA numbers. While the nutrients that GA represents are critically important, we can't rely on the GA to track them down.

A guarantee is only as good as the facts behind it

Knowing what's truly behind some pet food terminology is key to building a solid foundation. Once built, we won't be frustrated or misled by incomplete information like the GA numbers. We're able to understand which clues to trust and what to take with a grain of salt.

Guaranteed Analysis implies a guarantee, but is too general to use as a foundation for a true investigation. Stick to ingredient analysis and Feeding Guidelines to determine quality. The GA numbers should be seen for what they are—a crude method of comparing a range of factors that may, or may not, be in the bag.

Just as the guarantee behind the GA is questionable, so are pet food names. It's time to meet one final group of misleading monikers, pet food label names.

Captain K says:

"A guarantee is only as good as what's behind it.

GA presents a good front, but not much more.

Stick with feeding guidelines for a better indication of quality."

From the "Guaranteed Analysis" Evidence Archive:

Cindy walked into the store looking for a low protein food for her hyperactive hound. "I've heard that it helps to feed a lower protein food to dogs that have a lot of excess energy. I'm looking for something that has 18% or less protein."

This request seems easy enough to address by simply comparing protein percentages of the Guaranteed Analysis. But choosing a food on the basis of single GA number can be a risky strategy when other factors are ignored.

For starters, it's difficult to know for certain whether the excess energy and behavior issue is caused by high protein alone. Assuming it is, a simple drop in protein could indeed solve Cindy's problem.

But we've already seen that the GA numbers on a bag of food are not exact. Choosing a food with a GA of 18% Crude Protein does not ensure 18% useable protein, which is what Cindy wants. The useable protein in this bag of food may be higher or lower than 18%.

Since we can't be certain of the protein level, let's assume this particular food meets Cindy's requirement for a lower protein formula. We're not done yet: now it becomes important to consider how lowering the protein of a food can affect its nutritional value.

A dog's energy does not only come from protein. Some comes from from fat and carbohydrates in addition to protein. Lowering the protein level without considering the overall effect of calories from fat and carbs becomes counterproductive.

There's an important relationship between protein, fat and carbohydrates. When protein is lowered, a dog's body still needs energy to maintain vital functions. This energy may now come from a higher fat &/ or carbohydrate content in the food.

Choosing a lower protein food without comparing the fat and carb content can accidentally lead to a lower-calorie diet. This low-calorie diet may appear to solve a dog's hyperactivity problem. It can also swing things too far in the opposite direction by not meeting a dog's daily caloric needs.

When a food does not provide enough daily calories, a dog can become lethargic. While the dog may now appear calm, that could be the result of simply not having enough energy for basic needs. This is not a healthy situation.

While Cindy's desire to reduce protein may be a worthwhile goal, it cannot reliably be reached through a partial GA comparison. Fat content and other ingredients should be considered as well.

Choosing a food strictly on a single GA number is commonly done, but is misleading. Guaranteed Analysis is a vague guideline, rather than a guarantee of contents. The numbers should be viewed together as a whole, rather than as separate pieces. They serve a purpose, but are often interpreted incorrectly.

The same potential for misinterpretation can apply to pet food names unless we know what's behind that name.

Recognize Tips, Tricks and Traps of Labels:

How a Good System is Corrupted to Deceive Consumers

What do Lassie, Butch Cassidy and Deep Throat all have in common?

Every dog lover is familiar with Lassie. More than a half dozen male dogs, most notably Pal, have portrayed her in film and television roles. But the alias "Lassie" is the name we all recognize.

Our buddy Butch was born Robert Leroy Parker. He used more than seven other aliases during his notorious criminal career until his reported death in the early 1900s.

And Deep Throat? During the Watergate scandal, he became a household name tied to the resignation of a president. The true identity behind this alias remained hidden for more than 30 years. His tips helped expose deception, manipulation and cover-up in the highest levels of government.

We recognize Lassie, Butch Cassidy and Deep Throat as familiar aliases. Would it surprise you to find aliases on pet food labels? Let's use a bit of detective work to uncover the truth behind some familiar pet food names.

What's in a name?

Naming a pet food product may seem to be a fairly straight-forward exercise. We expect a pet food name to be honest about what's inside the product.

And so, we rely on pet food labeling regulations. These regulations are intended to protect the public by ensuring transparency, accuracy and compliance in product names.

But a truthful name is often not as appealing as a creative one. It's the creative names, or aliases, that can either hide or expose the truth depending on how we look at them.

Labels reveal their secrets once we know the code

We've already seen what's hidden in the Ingredient List and Feeding Guidelines. Now we're about to expose some of the secrets found in product names. We only need a few tips to see what's hiding behind their aliases.

First, a word of warning: this section is a bit more technical because we're examining regulatory guidelines. Recognizing the way names appear because of these guidelines is as amusing as it is instructive. While it's helpful to become familiar with these conventions, they certainly don't need to be memorized!

Pull up a chair, grab your beverage of choice, and get ready to roll your eyes. We'll be looking at four primary label naming guidelines including:

1. The 95% Rule
2. The 25% Rule (a/k/a the Dinner Rule)
3. The 3% Rule (a/k/a the Flavor Rule)
4. The "With" Rule

The 95% Rule is the most straightforward

This rule applies mainly to canned or raw foods using specific animal protein(s) in a name. It requires that the named animal ingredient(s) make up at least 95% of that food's weight.

For example, Slithering Snake for Dogs must contain at least 95% serpent by weight. And Chicken & Beef for Dogs must contain 95% chicken & beef by weight. Or so it seems.

The 95% measurement does not include the weight of any water or "condiments" used in processing. With this added moisture, the named animal ingredient(s) must make up at least 70% of the product.

As a result, the 95% Rule might more accurately be referred to as the 70% rule. This distinction may initially be challenging to grasp. Let it sit for a bit and it will become clear.

Our next labeling guideline also refers to different percentages when considering water used for processing.

The 25% Rule applies to both canned and dry foods

This rule is also known as "The Dinner Rule." It requires a "descriptive" term such as Dinner, Platter, Entree, Nuggets, Recipe, or Formula.

The descriptive terms are used when a name contains ingredients that make up at least 25%, but no more than 95% of a food. We see one of these descriptive terms on almost every dry dog food bag.

This range of 25%-95% also excludes moisture used in processing, and is NOT limited to animal ingredients.

The Dinner Rule gets a bit more convoluted when adjusting for moisture or multiple ingredients:

    a. A single ingredient used in the name must account for at least 10% of the formula weight without moisture.

b. If more than one ingredient is included in a formula name, the combination of all named ingredients, not including moisture, must total at least 25% of the product.

c. Any individually named ingredient in a combination formula name must be at least 3% of the total weight without moisture.

This is not as confusing as it may first appear

Rather than struggle with all the previous facts and figures, here's a simple way to recognize what's behind the 25% Rule.

- The 25% requirement applies when a single ingredient is used in a formula name.
- When multiple ingredients are named, each must consist of at least 3% and total at least 25%.

Denise's dog, Darby, was particularly fond of beef. When Denise spotted the new Beef & Rice Dinner for dogs on the shelf, she snatched a can to bring home for Darby.

Darby had previously shown a disdain for only two ingredients. For some reason, he just wouldn't touch anything made with chicken or egg. Denise thought it might have been the result of the Chicken & Egg food that made Darby sick when he was a puppy. Since then, it had been beef all the way.

So it came as a surprise that Darby sniffed around the bowl of this new food, turned up his nose, and walked away. Only then did Denise turn the can over to examine the ingredients of her new Beef & Rice Dinner for dogs:

BEEF BROTH, BEEF, CHICKEN, BEEF LIVER, CHICKEN LIVER, GROUND RICE, RICE BRAN, EGG PRODUCT, etc.

This particular formula may contain almost as much chicken as beef. It also contains egg. But this is a Beef & Rice formula—how can that be?

Remember the 25% Rule? Here the beef and the rice ingredients combine to make up at least 25% of the formula, so it's in compliance. In this case we could be looking at a weight of 13% beef and 12% rice. The actual amount of chicken and egg is anyone's guess. As is the makeup of that remaining 75%.

But we're not done yet. Think the Dinner Rule is convoluted? Let's see what comes next.

The 3% Rule is also known as the "With Rule"

The "With Rule" is one of the most creative uses of labeling we find in pet food. It allows a product name to contain an ingredient which is at least 3% of the total weight without water. This 3% ingredient appears following the word "with."

The "With Rule" was originally developed to allow manufacturers to boast of minor, but attractive, ingredients used in small amounts.

Under the original rule, these ingredients were not intended to be reflected in the name of a formula. Homestyle Dinner for Dogs might include an attractive display panel proudly proclaiming "Now with more Chicken and Vegetables!" somewhere on the package.

That has now changed to allow the "with" ingredients to be used as part of a formula name. This food may now be labeled as Homestyle Dinner for Dogs with Chicken and Vegetables.

A food name containing "with" may not contain much

There is a significant difference between "Chicken, Rice & Vegetable Dog Food" and "Dog Food with Chicken, Rice & Vegetables."

The first is governed by the 25% rule and may contain up to 94% Chicken. The second is governed by the "With Rule" and may contain only 3% Chicken. Think that's a bit far-fetched?

A clear case of the 3% Rule is found in this dog food with Chicken, Rice and Vegetables. It's why we have to dig down to the 7th ingredient before uncovering any Chicken, Rice or Vegetables.

GROUND WHOLE CORN, CORN GLUTEN MEAL, POULTRY BY-PRODUCT MEAL, MEAT AND BONE MEAL, ANIMAL FAT (preserved with BHA and Citric Acid), CHICKEN, BREWERS RICE, PEAS, etc.

We can easily recognize what's behind the alias of "with" because of the 3% rule. But there is one more alias to expose—"Flavored" Dog Food.

The "Flavor Rule" can be the most misleading of all

Under this final rule, there are no required percentage guidelines for the flavoring agent named in the formula. Not only are there no percentage requirements, there are no ingredient requirements!

Yes, you read that correctly.

A "Chicken Flavor" dog food is not required to contain any chicken at all. As long as the flavor is detectable, a "Flavor" claim may be used.

The flavor can be detected by lab analysis or animal tests. The standards are quite low, and the interpretation quite loose.

Here are two examples of "Beef Flavor" dog food which need no further explanation. The beef flavor included in the first product name comes from meat meal or animal digest.

CORN, SOYBEAN MEAL, MEAT AND BONE MEAL, WHEAT MIDDLINGS, ANIMAL FAT (PRESERVED WITH MIXED TOCOPHEROLS), ANIMAL DIGEST, SALT, CALCIUM CARBONATE, CELLULOSE GUM, WHEAT FLOUR...

This food uses meat meal, beef tallow or animal digest to provide its beef flavor.

GROUND YELLOW CORN, MEAT AND BONE MEAL, SOYBEAN MEAL, BEEF TALLOW PRESERVED WITH MIXED-TOCOPHEROLS (FORM OF VITAMIN E), CORN GLUTEN MEAL, EGG AND CHICKEN FLAVOR, ANIMAL DIGEST, SALT

As an ingredient, "Flavor" can include by-products or meal ingredients. As part of a product name, it is a red flag that immediately screams low quality.

111

Labeling guidelines were intended to help consumers

Labeling guidelines are clear to Dog Food Detectives who recognize an alias and understand its secrets. Many consumers are not aware of how product names can mislead.

Legal ambiguity exists with current naming rules. The true nature of some products is often hidden as a result.

Must we really understand all of these naming conventions?

By now you may be wondering, "Do I really need to know all this garbage? The DFD System wasn't supposed to require memorization or math."

Well, you're right. You don't need to know any of this. You can be a wonderfully effective DFD by just recognizing a deceptive label name. There's no need to remember the details of each rule.

Awareness of the "With" and "Flavor" rules now raises a red flag without committing any numbers to memory. The same applies to the descriptive names covered by the 25% rule. We understand what's behind the names using these familiar aliases.

A similar principle applies to our friend, Mark Felt. While many of us may be unfamiliar with the name, his Deep Throat alias is quite recognizable. We know exactly what he stood for without remembering all the details.

It's a cover-up, not a crime

Naming rules that were intended to clarify what's in a pet food can often mask the truth by using creative wording.

Understanding the meaning of product name aliases simplifies our investigation. We can now instantly uncover another common secret hiding on a pet food label.

Adding recognition of these pet food aliases to your skills completes the DFD System. Flip the page to review what's been covered. Then go forth and spread the word as a confident Dog Food Detective!

Captain K says:

"Foods don't need Flavors or Withs in their names.

Skip those and look for the understandable terms.

Then double check your choice on the Ingredient List."

From the "Label Deceptions" Evidence Archive:

Dog Food Detectives do not need checklists, but they do come in handy for pet food manufacturers when naming their products. A pet food name must meet AAFCO guidelines before it hits the market.

To help with this process, a handy checklist is available to ensure compliance. There are, however, a variety of ways to follow these guidelines and still create confusion for consumers. But not if we recognize some basic terms.

Here's an excerpt from the AAFCO Pet Food Regulation Label Review Checklist which addresses the requirements for names:

"95% Rule" — Regulation PF3(b)(1)
If an ingredient (or combination of ingredients) with no descriptive term(s) is part of the product name (Example: My Favorite Beef Dog Food):

1. Is/Are the named ingredient(s) derived from animals, poultry, or fish?

2. Is the formulation comprised of at least 95% of the named ingredient(s), exclusive of water sufficient for processing, in the formulation?

3. Is the same name listed in the ingredient statement?

114

4. If multiple ingredients are listed, are they in the same order in both product name and ingredient statement and is each ingredient at least 3% of formula?

5. Are all ingredients that are included in the product name printed in the same size, style and color print?

"25% Rule" — Regulation PF3(b)(2)

If an ingredient is part of the product name and is listed with a primary descriptor term such as dinner, entree, formula, etc. (Example: My Favorite Salmon Entree Cat Food):

1. Is the ingredient at least 25% of the formulation, exclusive of water sufficient for processing?

2. If more than one ingredient is named, is each ingredient at least 3% the formulation, with named ingredients totaling at least 25% of the formulation? (Example: My Favorite Beef, Chicken and Lamb Dinner Dog Food)

3. Are the names listed in ingredient statement?

4. Are they in the same order in both the product name and ingredient list?

5. Are all ingredients and primary descriptor that are included in the product name printed in same size, style and color print?

"With Rule" — Regulation PF3(c)

If there is an ingredient name in the product name that includes a descriptor term such as "with" (Example: My Favorite Dog Food With Beet):

1. Does each ingredient named constitute at least 3% of the formulation exclusive of water sufficient for processing?

2. Are they in the same order in both the product name and ingredient list?

3. Is the word "with" in the same size, style, color and case print as the ingredients that are included in the product name?

4. Does the product name meet the print size specification listed below?
   (Panel size area; Maximum types size for "with" detail)
   <5 sq. inches; 1/8 inch height
   5-25 sq. inches; 1/4 inch height
   25-100 sq. inches; 3/8 inch height
   100-400 sq. inches; 1/2 inch height
   400 sq. inches; 1 inch height

"Flavors Rule" — Regulation PF3(d)

If there is an ingredient named as a flavor (Example: My Favorite Chicken Flavor(ed) Dog Food):

1. Is this flavor source listed in the ingredient statement and if name is different is the flavor source identified?

2. Is the word "flavor(ed)" the same size type and as conspicuous as the name of the flavor designation in the product name?

As you can see, there are not many hurdles to overcome before using "With" or "Flavor" in a pet food name. These terms are attractive to us, but are relatively meaningless when explaining what's truly contained in a food.

Label names bring us to the end of our third step of the System. Let's do a quick review before wrapping up and considering the Closing Arguments.

Summary: Step 3
Engage the Hidden Players

- Pay attention to Feeding Guidelines. They are your mailbox chalk marks.

- Lower Feeding Guidelines will usually mean a more highly digestible food. Better-quality foods have lower Feeding Guidelines.

- Better-quality foods usually offer better value than lower-quality foods.

- You will feed less of a more digestible food. This is why a more expensive food may cost less to feed than a cheaper bag of food.

- Guaranteed Analysis should not be used to judge the quality or value of a food. The GA numbers represent a range of values, not specific numbers.

- Guaranteed Analysis numbers represent crude levels of nutrients, not useable levels.

- Pet food names can be an early sign of a low quality food. Look closely at the ingredients of foods that include "with" or "flavor" in the actual product name.

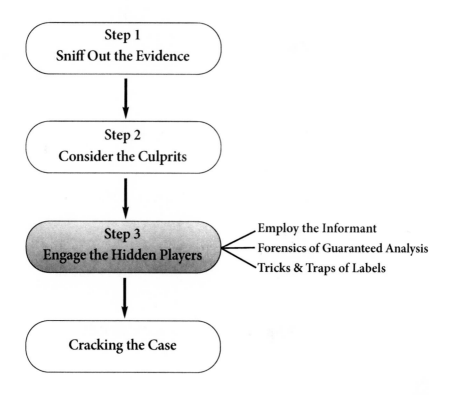

We're now ready to present our Closing Arguments and put all of the System steps together to reach a verdict.

Cracking the Case

1. Sniff
Money • Distractions
Special Needs

2. Consider
Interrogate • Splitting
Meat vs. Meal

3. Engage
Feeding Guidelines
GA • Labels

Closing Arguments
Render Your Verdict

Closing Arguments:
Summing up the Evidence

Go ahead and take a deep breath. Our detective training is coming to an end, and it's almost time to test our skills in the field.

We've visited a host of seemingly disconnected cases during our dietary dragnet. Each step revealed clues which moved us closer to the goal of finding the best food for our pet. Before we render a verdict, let's do a quick review of our 3-step journey through the Dog Food Detective System.

1. Sniff out the evidence by eliminating distractions
2. Identify and interrogate the usual ingredient suspects
3. Use informants to uncover disguises and reveal the true cost of a food

We began with a quick glance at the Ingredient List to reveal the most obvious clues.

1. Sniff out the evidence by eliminating distractions

Ingredients tell us many things, but they can't tell us everything. We first set a budget range and identify any ingredients we'd like to avoid. We're now left with a smaller group of foods to evaluate.

This group gets narrowed down even further if we're looking for something in particular, or have other personal preferences to consider. If there are no additional requirements, a simple glance at each bag lets the food begin to speak for itself.

2. Identify and interrogate the usual ingredient suspects

By examining the first six ingredients for specific meat proteins and whole ingredients we begin to reveal the true nature of a food.

Now we can easily spot any red flags. These include foods with generic meats, by-products, split ingredients and chemical preservatives.

By questioning the form and source of ingredients, we're left with a short list of options. These foods warrant a closer look.

3. Use informants to uncover the masters of disguise and reveal the true cost of a food

Feeding Guidelines are an overlooked, underused and absolutely essential informant which helps reveal the true quality and value of a food.

Feeding Guidelines reflect the quality of the ingredients, which directly relate to the value and digestibility of a food.

Remember these tips, which are at the heart of your System:
- A pet food cannot use poor quality ingredients and also be highly digestible.
- A highly digestible food uses higher-quality ingredients.
- Smaller amounts of a highly digestible food provide your dog adequate daily nutrition.
- The less food required, the lower the Feeding Guidelines.
- The lower the Feeding Guidelines, the more digestible the food.

A highly digestible, better-quality food is easier on your dog's system. This leads to better overall health for your pet. Less food also means less waste for you to clean up, so you'll have more energy as well!

Feeding Guidelines are always consulted by Dog Food Detectives before rendering a verdict. They offer critical evidence about a food's quality and value. The guidelines also reveal the true cost of our pet food.

Our verdict reflects the true or hidden cost of feeding

When we feed less of a better quality food, the bag lasts longer. When the bag lasts longer, our daily cost is reduced.

We may pay more upfront for a better food, but the cost over time is less. One bag of $60 food that lasts 30 days is a better value than a $30 bag of food that disappears in less than two weeks. Looking at just the price tag without regard for how long the bag will last is a common oversight to avoid.

It's simple to compare the cost of two foods with the same Feeding Guidelines. When the guidelines are different, a quick math exercise can reveal if a more expensive food costs less to feed. Visit Appendix #1 for examples of how to calculate this cost.

CAPTAIN K'S
Case File

"Figuring out the ingredients was hard (i.e. meal vs. dehydrated, etc.)," said Marina. "But I realized that my main issue was that I had no clue what the nutritional requirements were for a dog. How much protein, fat, carbs, or vitamins are ideal vs. minimum requirements or maximum values? Heck, I didn't even know how many calories to aim for!"

This can be a concern among pet parents. Although the AAFCO Guidelines provide a starting point, developing a deeper understanding remains a challenge that the DFD System does not address.

These types of questions move beyond the basic foundation we've built with the System. At this point, we may want to consider more high-quality food options like home-prepared diets or raw feeding. Some excellent resources for these types of food can be found in the Bibliography.

One of the bonuses included with The Dog Food Detective is a list of selected AAFCO Nutrient Profiles for pet food. These are provided as a reference only, and give you a broad overview of what AAFCO considers adequate. Should you choose to continue your detective training and venture deeper into the delightful world of nutrition, this may offer a good starting point.

Pet food nutrition is a fascinating subject

As newly certified Dog Food Detectives, we've barely scratched the surface of pet food nutrition. We've achieved our goal of learning to quickly evaluate and choose appropriate foods, but there's always much more to learn.

Mastering the DFD System lays an excellent foundation, and may be all that's needed to face mountains of misleading marketing with a smile. For many pet parents, and pet shop employees, this System will be your secret weapon to help support a healthy and affordable feeding program.

Want to continue your pet food education? You'll find some DFD System exercises in Appendix #1. The names and full Ingredient List for all foods used as examples in this book are shown in Appendix #2.

If you've read this far and have completed the exercises, you're to be congratulated. Send an email with "I'm Certifiable" in the subject line to craig@dog-food-detective.com and include any questions or comments you may have. You'll receive answers to any of your questions, along with a personalized Certificate of Course Completion, suitable for framing or lining litter boxes.

Congratulations on becoming a Dog Food Detective!

Afterword
Render Your Verdict

We're all familiar with detectives from movies and television shows. There's one thing they all have in common. Once their investigation is complete, they hand over their work to others so a verdict can be reached.

These detectives turn over their case files to attorneys. Their evidence is presented to a judge and jury who render a final verdict. Our System is quite different.

We use an independent source to confirm our conclusion

The "best" food we uncover using the System may not always be the right choice. We can't know for sure until it is endorsed by our canine companion.

In rare cases when the initial verdict is appealed by our dog, it's easy to spot the evidence: food left in the bowl, softer stool, more shedding, dull coat or constant scratching.

We can easily reverse a decision, even after passing judgement. We can admit more evidence into the case, or choose another suspect from the Step 1 short list of foods. The beauty of the DFD System is its flexibility to easily adapt to these kinds of changes.

Let's play with the System!

Now that our Dog Food Detective training is complete, we don't want our newly acquired abilities to grow stale. To ensure our DFD skills remain fresh, let's do our own version of the detective's refresher class.

Appendix #1 presents a few common cases for the DFD System. These cases demonstrate the flexibility of the System when faced with four different priorities:

1. Budget
2. Personal preference
3. Quality
4. Value

All the clues in these cases were obtained from a single retailer, for dog foods currently on the market. The clues are provided in the form of Ingredient Lists, Feeding Guidelines and purchase price.

We'll apply the steps of the System to see how changes in priority can affect the verdict in each case.

Flip to Appendix #1 and begin with budget, since that will almost always play a role in our final verdict. In the first case, it is the primary factor.

Acknowledgments

This book would not have been possible without the help from members of the Smiley Dog family, whose questions provided the stories for this book and continue to inspire curiosity.

A debt of gratitude is owed to Dan Ginsburg, whose principles and passion for nutritional excellence offered a beacon through a convoluted industry. To Leigh and Ron Briggs who graciously shared their knowledge long before this detective journey began.

Thank you to Sean d'Souza and the team in the Cave at 5000bc for the inspiration to share information in ways that benefit many. To Philip Riggs for his light hearted illustrations, Trisha Cupra for her eye-catching cover design, and Lizabet Nix as editor who thankfully pushed for improvements even as I pushed back.

To my partner in life, Barbara Sanderson, whose feedback helped clarify the direction of the project.

To Eric Brotman for his insightful assistance as an early reader.

And to Mom and Dad who, despite skepticism, encouraged the vision as they have always done.

And perhaps most of all, for the dogs.

Woof!

Appendix #1
Dog Food Detective System™ Exercises

Here are a handful of real life cases ripped from today's pet food shelves. Use your newly acquired DFD skills to see what your System reveals.

Choose from any of the seven cases and apply the DFD System to solve the question it asks. You can work through all seven in order, or choose only those that suit your needs.

Some cases require the investigation of a single piece of evidence like the Ingredient List. Others require two or more steps of your System to be combined.

At the end of each case you'll see how well your answers match up with Captain K's. The solution is found at the end of each case. First, the case preview:

Case #1: The Budget Buster
Which of these foods is the most expensive to feed?

Case #2: The Budget Friend
Which of these foods is the cheapest to feed?

Case #3: The Grain Drain
Which food without wheat or corn will last the longest?

Case #4: Sniffing out Quality
Which of these foods has the best quality ingredients?

Case #5: Friend or Foe?
List the foods in order of quality of ingredients.

Case #6: The Vanishing Act
Which bag of food will disappear more quickly than the others?

Case #7: The Value Revealed by the System
Which of these foods offers the best Value?(Value is based on quality and cost)

Now for the suspects. There are six suspects and each has an Ingredient List, Feeding Guidelines, bag size and purchase price to help you sniff out the answers.

The following guidelines apply to all six suspects:

- Ingredient Lists were accurate at the time of publication (some changed dramatically while this book was being written!)
- Feeding Guidelines are simplified to an average measurement when needed (3 to 4 cups becomes 3.5 cups for these exercises)
- Feeding Guidelines recommendations for "least active" are assumed ("least active" requires less food)
- The largest bag size available of each food is used
- Pricing for all suspects was obtained from a single retail outlet
- Brands of all suspects are nationally available

A suspect cheat sheet could be useful as you solve these cases. Your cheat sheet should include suspect number, bag size, purchase price, and feeding guidelines. You could also include the first six ingredients to avoid having to refer back to the full suspect lineup during your investigations.

(If you'd like to know the brand names of these suspects, they can be found at the end of this section.)

Meet our suspects on the following page and begin gathering evidence to crack one or more of these cases.

Good luck! Here's your suspect lineup:

Suspect #1

Chicken, Corn Meal, Ground Whole Grain Sorghum, Chicken By-Product Meal, Dried Beet Pulp, Chicken Flavor, Chicken Fat (preserved with mixed Tocopherols, a source of Vitamin E), Dried Egg Product, Potassium Chloride, Salt, Caramel, Flax Meal, Calcium Carbonate, Choline Chloride, Fructooligosaccharides, Vitamins (Vitamin E Supplement, Ascorbic Acid, Vitamin A Acetate, Calcium Pantothenate, Biotin, Thiamine Mononitrate (source of vitamin B1), Vitamin B12 Supplement, Niacin, Riboflavin Supplement (source of vitamin B2), Inositol, Pyridoxine Hydrochloride (source of vitamin B6), Vitamin D3 Supplement, Folic Acid), Minerals (Ferrous Sulfate, Zinc Oxide, Manganese Sulfate, Copper Sulfate, Manganous Oxide, Potassium Iodide, Cobalt Carbonate), L-Lysine Monohydrochloride, DL-Methionine, Brewers Dried Yeast, L-Carnitine, Rosemary Extract

Largest size: 29.1 lb bag
Purchase price: $42.50
Protein (min): 25%
Fat (min): 14%
Fiber (max): 4%
Moisture (max): 10%
Feeding Guidelines for 50-pound dog: 2.5 cups

Suspect #2

Chicken Meal, Ground Brown Rice, Rice Bran, Chicken Fat (preserved with Mixed Tocopherols and Ascorbyl Palmitate), Oatmeal, Beet Pulp, Flaxseed, Fish Meal, Chicken Cartilage (Source of Glucosamine and Chondroitin Sulfate), Natural Chicken Flavor, Sunflower Oil, Menhaden Fish Oil, Potassium Chloride, Salt, Dicalcium Phosphate, Choline Chloride, Calcium Ascorbate (source of Vitamin C), Zinc Amino Acid Chelate, Iron Amino Acid Chelate, Dried Lactobacillus acidophilus Fermentation Product, Dried Enterococcus faecium Fermentation Product, Yucca Schidigera

Extract, Biotin, Manganese Amino Acid Chelate, Cobalt Amino Acid Chelate, Calcium Carbonate, Vitamin E Supplement, Vitamin A Supplement, Calcium Pantothenate, Niacin, Pyridoxine Hydrochloride (B6), Thiamine Mononitrate (B1), Vitamin B12 Supplement, Vitamin D3 Supplement, Riboflavin Supplement, DL-Methionine, Copper Amino Acid Chelate, Folic Acid, Selenium Yeast, Calcium Iodate.

Largest size: 40 lb bag
Purchase price: $58.75
Protein (min): 24%
Fat (min): 14%
Fiber (max): 3.5%
Moisture (max): 10%
Feeding Guidelines for 50-pound dog: 2 cups

Suspect #3

Chicken, Chicken Meal, Whole Brown Rice, Brewers Rice, Rice Bran, Whole Grain Oatmeal, Chicken Fat (preserved with mixed Tocopherols), Natural Flavor, Pea Protein, Dried Plain Beet Pulp, Sunflower Oil (preserved with mixed Tocopherols), Soybean Oil (preserved with mixed Tocopherols), Potassium Chloride, Choline Chloride, DL-Methionine, Salt, Vitamin E Supplement, Zinc Sulfate, Niacin Supplement, L-Ascorbyl-2-Polyphosphate (source of Vitamin C), Calcium Pantothenate, Riboflavin Supplement (Vitamin B2), Pyridoxine Hydrochloride (Vitamin B6), Vitamin B12 Supplement, Copper Proteinate, Iron Proteinate, Selenium Yeast, Biotin, Manganese Proteinate, Vitamin A Supplement, Potassium Iodide, Thiamine Mononitrate (Vitamin B1), Vitamin D3 Supplement, Folic Acid, Rosemary Extract, Decaffeinated Green Tea Extract, Spearmint Extract

Largest size: 30 lb bag
Purchase price: $59.75
Protein (min): 22%
Fat (min): 14%
Fiber (max): 3.5%
Moisture (max): 10%
Feeding Guidelines for 55-pound dog: 3.75 cups

Suspect #4

Chicken, Brewers Rice, Whole Grain Wheat, Poultry By-Product
Meal (natural source of glucosamine), Corn Gluten Meal, Animal
Fat preserved with Mixed-Tocopherols (form of Vitamin E), Whole
Grain Corn, Soy Flakes, Soybean Meal, Fish Meal (natural source
of glucosamine), Animal Digest, Glycerin, Dried Egg Product,
Wheat Bran, Salt, Calcium Carbonate, Calcium Phosphate,
Potassium Chloride, Zinc Proteinate, Vitamin E Supplement,
Choline Chloride, Manganese Proteinate, Ferrous Sulfate, Sulfur,
L-Ascorbyl-2-Polyphosphate (source of Vitamin C), Niacin,
Copper Proteinate, Vitamin A Supplement, Calcium Pantothenate,
Thiamine Mononitrate, Riboflavin Supplement, Vitamin B-12
Supplement, Pyridoxine Hydrochloride, Garlic Oil, Folic Acid,
Vitamin D-3 Supplement, Calcium Iodate, Biotin, Menadione
Sodium Bisulfite Complex (source of Vitamin K activity),
Sodium Selenite.

Largest size: 35 lb bag
Purchase price: $55.50
Protein (min): 26%
Fat (min): 16%
Fiber (max): 3%
Moisture (max): 12%
Feeding Guidelines for 50-pound dog: 3 cups

Suspect #5

Chicken, Whole Grain Wheat, Brewers Rice, Whole Grain
Sorghum, Corn Gluten Meal, Whole Grain Corn, Chicken Meal,
Chicken Liver Flavor, Pork Fat, Dried Beet Pulp, Soybean Oil,
Lactic Acid, Flaxseed, Potassium Chloride, Iodized Salt, Choline
Chloride, Calcium Carbonate, vitamins (Vitamin E Supplement,
L-Ascorbyl-2-Polyphosphate (source of vitamin C), Niacin
Supplement, Thiamine Mononitrate, Vitamin A Supplement,
Calcium Pantothenate, Biotin, Vitamin B12 Supplement,
Pyridoxine Hydrochloride, Riboflavin Supplement, Folic Acid,
Vitamin D3 Supplement), minerals (Ferrous Sulfate, Zinc Oxide,
Copper Sulfate, Manganous Oxide, Calcium Iodate, Sodium
Selenite), Taurine, Oat Fiber, Mixed Tocopherols for freshness,
Phosphoric Acid, Beta-Carotene, Natural Flavors, Dried Apples,
Dried Broccoli, Dried Carrots, Dried Cranberries, Dried Peas

Largest size: 38.5 lb bag
Purchase price: $59.75
Protein (min): 21%
Fat (min): 12.5%
Fiber (max): 3%
Moisture (max): 10%
Feeding Guidelines for 50-pound dog: 3.125 cups

Suspect #6

Chicken, Chickpeas, Peas, Dried Eggs, Barley, Oats, Chicken Fat
(preserved with mixed tocopherols), Dicalcium Phosphate,
Quinoa, Sun-Cured Alfalfa, Flaxseed, Natural Flavors, Calcium
Carbonate, Salt, Spinach, Sweet Potatoes, Tomato Pomace,
Potassium Chloride, Choline Chloride, Blueberries, Cranberries,
Apricots, Carrots, Zinc Proteinate, Iron Proteinate, Copper
Proteinate, Manganese Proteinate, Sodium Selenite, Calcium
Iodate, Vitamin E Supplement, Thiamine Mononitrate, Niacin

Supplement, Calcium Pantothenate, Biotin, Vitamin A Supplement, Riboflavin Supplement, Vitamin B12 Supplement, Pyridoxine Hydrochloride, Vitamin D3 Supplement, Folic Acid, Dandelion Greens, Chicory Root Extract, Mixed Tocopherols (preservative), Rosemary Extract.

Largest size: 26 lb bag
Purchase price: $68.75
Protein (min): 24.5%
Fat (min): 15%
Fiber (max): 5%
Moisture (max): 10%
Feeding Guidelines for 50-pound dog: 3 cups

Now that we've seen our suspects, let's move on to the actual cases. Remember, Captain K's solution is found at the end of each case.

Let's start by following the money!

Case #1: The Budget Buster
Which of these foods is the most expensive to feed?

To solve this case, we consider the tips from our primary informant lurking within the Feeding Guidelines. We can compare price per pound, cost per cup or cups per bag but that won't reveal the true cost.

Remember, it's the combination of Feeding Guidelines and purchase price that uncovers the true cost of feeding. Using our "Rule of Paw" from the Informant Evidence Archive, we'll say there are 3 cups per pound.

Suspects #3 and #5 have the highest Feeding Guidelines, so we'll begin with them to set a baseline. Quite often, the foods with the highest Feeding Guidelines cost the most to feed over time. Let's see if that turns out to be true in this case.

Suspect #3 Investigation
3.75 cups for a 55-pound dog
Cost of 30 lb bag- $59.75
Let's be generous and round this off to feeding 3.5 cups for a 50-pound dog. We can always revisit this if needed.

30 lb bag X 3 cups/ pound= 90 cups in the bag
90 cups @ $59.75= $0.66/ cup
Daily feeding cost of 3.5 cups/ day is 3.5 X $0.66= $2.31/ day

Suspect #5 Investigation
3.125 cups for 50-pound dog
Cost of 38.5 lb bag- $59.75

38.5 lb X 3 cups/ pound= 115.5 cups in the bag
115.5 cups @ $59.75= $0.52/ cup
Daily feeding cost of 3.125 cups is 3.125 X $0.52 or $1.63/ day

This range of daily feeding costs is quite large for two bags of food priced just about the same. It results from the different bag sizes and Feeding Guidelines. Now let's see what happens when we look at the other suspects.

Suspect #1 Investigation
2.5 cups for a 50-pound dog
Cost of 29.1 lb bag- $42.50

29.1 lb X 3 cups/ pound= 87.3 cups in the bag
87.3 cups @ $42.50 = $0.49 /cup
Daily feeding cost of 2.5 cups is 2.5 X $0.49 or $1.23/ day

Suspect #2 Investigation
2 cups for a 50-pound dog
Cost of 40 lb bag- $58.75

40 lb X 3 cups/ pound= 120 cups in the bag
120 cups @ $58.75 = $0.49 /cup
Daily feeding cost of 2 cups= $0.98/ day

Suspect #4 Investigation
3 cups for a 50-pound dog
Cost of 35 lb bag- $55.50

35 lb X 3 cups/ pound= 105 cups in the bag
105 cups @ $55.50 = $0.53 /cup
Daily feeding cost of 3 cups= $1.59/ day

Suspect #6 Investigation
3 cups for a 50-pound dog
Cost of 26 lb bag- $68.75

26 lb X 3 cups/ pound= 78 cups in the bag
78 cups @ $68.75 = $0.88 /cup
Daily feeding cost of 3 cups= $2.64/ day

The Verdict:
The spendiest food? Suspect #6 at $2.64/ day.

Even though Suspect #6 didn't have the highest Feeding Guidelines, its small bag size, high purchase price and relatively high Feeding Guidelines combine to make it the costliest to feed.

Case #2: The Budget Friend
Which of these foods is the cheapest to feed?

The previous case took far too much math, so let's cut ourselves a break here. The same calculations we used for Case #1 can be applied to solve this one.

Already solved Case #1? Great—refer to that answer and you'll have the solution for this one as well! If you have not solved the previous Case, the same steps apply:

- Use the bag size to calculate number of cups per bag (3 cups per pound)
- Use the purchase price to calculate price per cup (purchase price divided by number of cups in the bag)
- Multiply the Feeding Guidelines by the cost per cup

This gives us the daily cost of feeding.

The Verdict:
The most budget friendly food? Clearly Suspect #2 at just $0.98/ day

Case #3: The Grain Drain
Which food without wheat or corn will last the longest?

Our first step is to eliminate the foods that contain wheat or corn.

140

A quick scan removes Suspects 1, 4 and 5 from our list.

We now look at the tip supplied by our trusty Informant for the remaining suspects. The Feeding Guidelines are:

Suspect #2 – 2 cups
Suspect #3 – 3.75 cups
Suspect #6 – 3 cups

The Verdict:
Suspect #2 will last longer than any of the other wheat and corn-free formulas.

Suspect #2 has the lowest Feeding Guidelines. Less food fed each day means that bag will last longest.

It also comes in a 40 lb bag instead of the smaller 26 and 30 lb sizes of the other suspects.

Case #4: Sniffing out Quality
Which of these foods has the best quality ingredients?

At first glance, Suspect #6 appears to be the hands down favorite. It uses what appears to be whole ingredients except for those dried eggs. A problem is that fresh chicken leads the list, and isn't followed by another meat protein source. Chickpeas, peas and egg appear to provide the balance of the protein, which may not be ideal.

Suspect #3 reads fairly well, following a fresh chicken ingredient with chicken meal. But it follows that with a whole lot of grain, so a deeper investigation will be necessary. We'll need to check in with our informant hiding in the Feeding Guidelines to see whether this suspect is a poser or the real thing.

Suspect #2 could be a contender here as well. It's possible there's more rice here than chicken meal. A few other decent whole ingredients are included in oats and flaxseed, but now we're getting deeper into the list than we may want. Again, a consult with our informant in the Feeding Guidelines will be able to help us here.

The Verdict:
Without looking any further, Suspect #6 takes this case.

Whole ingredients, recognizable forms and names are what we like to see in a food. But we can't leave things here without applying the rest of the system.

Case #5: Friend or Foe?
List the foods in order of quality of ingredients

This case is a bit simpler. We already started this process of elimination during Case #4. Strictly on the basis of ingredient quality, these last three suspects are in a different category than the first three. Here's how they stack up – best appearing first:

1. Suspect #6
2. Suspect #2
3. Suspect #3
4. Suspect #5
5. Suspect #1
6. Suspect #4

Why did we cut Suspects 1, 4 and 5 loose? They didn't measure up to the others for the following reasons:

Suspect #1 flaws:
- Lots of grain in the first six ingredients
- Corn Meal follows the fresh meat ingredient listed first

- no additional meat protein until Chicken by-product meal in the fourth position
- Corn Meal and Chicken by-product meal as main protein sources

Suspect #4 flaws:

- a split ingredient in the second position—not what we want to see following a fresh meat ingredient
- another grain and the red flag of a generic by-product meal ingredient comes next
- not another decent ingredient until Fish Meal as #10— by then it's too little, too late

Suspect #5 flaws:

- Fresh ingredient is a good start
- Fresh ingredient is followed by less than ideal characters
- Whole ingredients in wheat, sorghum and corn
- Mixed with fraction of rice
- Chicken meal does not make an appearance until ingredient #7, leaving us with little animal protein

---

Case #6: The Vanishing Act
Which bag of food will last the longest?

For this case, we rely entirely on our informant in the Feeding Guidelines. Using those tips will quickly let us know how long each of these suspects will stick around. Here's how we proceed:

- Take the size of the bag in pounds
- Multiply the bag size by 3 cups/ pound to find the total number of cups in the bag
- Divide the total number of cups in the bag by the Feeding Guideline number for our 50-pound test dog

The steps in this case are very similar to what we did to solve Cases #1 and #2.

Let's see what this reveals:

Suspect #1
Bag size: 29.1 lb
Number of cups in the bag: 87.3 cups
Feeding Guidelines: 2.5 cups
Number of days the bag will last: 35 days

Suspect #2
Bag size: 40 lb
Number of cups in the bag: 120 cups
Feeding Guidelines: 2 cups
Number of days the bag will last: 60 days

Suspect #3
Bag size: 30 lb
Number of cups in the bag: 90 cups
Feeding Guidelines: 3.5 cups
Number of days the bag will last: 25.7 days

Suspect #4
Bag size: 35 lb
Number of cups in the bag: 105 cups
Feeding Guidelines: 3 cups
Number of days the bag will last: 35 days

Suspect #5
Bag size: 38.5 lb
Number of cups in the bag: 115.5 cups
Feeding Guidelines: 3.125 cups
Number of days the bag will last: 37 days

Suspect #6
Bag size: 26 lb
Number of cups in the bag: 78 cups
Feeding Guidelines: 3 cups
Number of days the bag will last: 26 days

The Verdict:
Suspect #2 is the clear winner at 60 days.

Looks like Suspect #3 takes the bottom spot, barely edged out by Suspect #6.

That's always good to know, but let's see how this verdict relates to the money in our pocket with the final case.

Case #7: The Value Revealed by the System
Which of these foods offer the best Value?
(Value is based on quality and cost)

Okay, I'll admit it. This is a bit of a trick question. Value is a pretty subjective judgement call. You may put a higher value on bottom line cost, and someone else may put a higher value on quality of ingredients. This exercise lets you do either. Or both.

There are no additional calculations needed for this Case. It's simply a matter of referring back to your previous answers. Whether you realize it or not, you've now successfully worked the entire system!

- We've looked at ingredients to determine which foods are the highest quality in Cases #4 and #5

- We've looked at digestibility by using Feeding Guidelines to determine how much food gets fed in Case #6

- We've looked the true cost of feeding in Cases #1 and #2

- We've looked at personal preferences in Case #3

Put these answers together in whatever combination is most important to you, and the best value will be revealed. For my pups, I'd certainly start with Suspect #2, despite the tempting ingredients listed by Suspect #6. The combination of ingredients, digestibility and price make this a clear winner for my value criteria.

Prefer a softer food—one with more moisture content? Suspect #6 is the only contender with higher than 10% moisture. Sure, you're paying for water content, but this suspect offers the best value if a soft texture is important to you.

Curious to know where your food falls within this system?

Perhaps your pet's food was used in these cases. If you'd like to know the true identity of these suspects, just keep reading. You'll find the full formula name and a link to the manufacturer's website on the next page.

**The following foods appeared in Appendix #1 Cases.
Their names were changed to protect the author.**

All links, pricing, Ingredient Lists, Feeding Guidelines, and Guaranteed
Analysis were current at the time of publication.

Suspect #1
Iams® ProActive Health Adult Chunks
The Iams® Company (a division of Procter and Gamble)
www.pg.com/en_US/index.shtml

Suspect #2
Precise® Naturals Chicken Meal and Rice Foundation Formula
Precise® Pet Products (a division of Texas Farm Products)
www.texasfarm.com

Suspect #3
Natural Choice® Wholesome Essentials Adult Chicken,
Whole Brown Rice & Oatmeal Formula
The Nutro® Company (a division of Mars, Inc.)
www.mars.com/global/brands/petcare.aspx

Suspect #4
ProPlan® Savor Adult Shredded Blend Chicken & Rice Formula
ProPlan® (a division of Nestlé Purina PetCare Co.)
www.nestlepurina.com

Suspect #5
Science Diet® Adult Advanced Fitness Original
Hills® Science Diet® (a division of Colgate-Palmolive Co.)
www.colgatepalmolive.com/app/Colgate/US/CompanyHomePage.cvsp

Suspect #6
Spring Naturals™ Chicken Dinner with Chickpeas, Quinoa & Berries
Performance Pet Products (a division of American Foods Group)
www.americanfoodsgroup.com

Appendix #2
Supporting References

Scattered throughout this book are examples of Ingredient Lists. Perhaps you've wondered if these were contrived to prove a point, or taken from food on the shelf.

Wonder no more. What follows are the actual formula names and the full Ingredient Lists. There is no shortage of supporting evidence available—these just happened to be the most conveniently available to support the information presented.

Chapter Two: Consider the Culprits
Spot the Suspects Ingredient List examples

The first, grain heavy example is:
ProPlan Chicken and Rice Adult

Ingredients: Chicken, Brewers Rice, Whole Grain Wheat, Corn Gluten Meal, Whole Grain Corn, Poultry By-Product Meal (natural source of glucosamine), Animal Fat preserved with Mixed-Tocopherols (form of Vitamin E), Barley, Corn Germ Meal, Fish Meal (natural source of glucosamine), Animal Digest, Fish Oil, Wheat Bran, Dried Egg Product, Calcium Phosphate, Salt, Potassium Chloride, Potassium Citrate, Vitamin E Supplement, Choline Chloride, L-Lysine Monohydrochloride, Zinc Sulfate, Ferrous Sulfate, L-ascorbyl-2-polyphosphate (source of Vitamin C), Manganese Sulfate, Niacin, Vitamin A Supplement, Calcium Carbonate, Copper Sulfate, Calcium Pantothenate, Garlic Oil, Pyridoxine Hydrochloride, Vitamin B-12 Supplement, Thiamine Mononitrate, Riboflavin Supplement, Calcium Iodate, Vitamin D-3 Supplement, Menadione Sodium Bisulfite Complex (source of Vitamin K activity), Folic Acid, Biotin, Sodium Selenite.

The second, more meat example is:
Nature's Variety Prairie Chicken & Brown Rice Recipe

Ingredients: Chicken, Chicken Meal, Oatmeal, Brown Rice, Barley, Chicken Fat (preserved with Mixed Tocopherols and Citric Acid), Sun-Cured Alfalfa Meal, Peas, Turkey Meal, Ground Flaxseed, Natural Chicken Flavor, Menhaden Fish Meal, Montmorillonite Clay, Carrots, Salt, Sweet Potatoes, Apples, Blueberries, Cranberries, Vitamins (Vitamin A Supplement, Vitamin D3 Supplement, Vitamin E Supplement, Niacin Supplement, d-Calcium Pantothenate, L-Ascorbyl-2-Polyphosphate, Thiamine Mononitrate, Pyridoxine Hydrochloride, Riboflavin Supplement, Folic Acid, Biotin, Vitamin B12 Supplement), Minerals (Zinc Proteinate, Iron Proteinate, Copper Proteinate, Manganese Proteinate, Ethylenediamine Dihydriodide, Sodium Selenite), Choline Chloride, Potassium Chloride, Yeast Culture, Dried Enterococcus faecium Fermentation Product, Dried Lactobacillus acidophilus Fermentation Product, Dried Aspergillus niger Fermentation Extract, Dried Trichoderma longibrachiatum Fermentation Extract, Dried Bacillus subtilis Fermentation Extract, Freeze Dried Chicken, Freeze Dried Turkey, Freeze Dried Turkey Liver, Freeze Dried Turkey Heart, Pumpkinseeds, Butternut Squash, Broccoli, Lettuce, Spinach, Dried Kelp, Salmon Oil, Apple Cider Vinegar, Parsley, Honey, Olive Oil, Alfalfa Sprouts, Persimmons, Inulin, Rosemary, Sage, Clove, Rosemary Extract.

The third, meat heavy example is:
Tuscan Naturals Harvest Turkey & Chicken Recipe

Ingredients: Turkey, Chicken, Chicken Meal, Lentils, Yellow Peas, Whitefish Meal, Brown Rice, Rice, Chicken Fat (preserved with mixed tocopherols), Flax Seed, Olive Oil (preserved with mixed tocopherols), Natural Flavor, Brewers Dried Yeast, Dicalcium Phosphate, Calcium Carbonate, Sweet Potatoes, Chicory Root

Extract, Salmon Oil (preserved with mixed tocopherols), Dried Kelp, Apples, Blueberries, Carrots, Alfafa Leaf, Vitamin E Supplement, Niacin Supplement, d-Calcium Pantothenate, Vitamin B-12 Supplement, Vitamin A Acetate, Vitamin D-3 Supplement, d-Biotin, Riboflavin Supplement, Thiamine Mononitrate, Pyridoxine Hydrochloride, Folic Acid, Iron Proteinate, Zinc Proteinate, Manganese Proteinate, Copper Proteinate, Sodium Selenite, Cobalt Protenate, Ethylenediamine Dihydroiodide, Dried Lactobacillus Acidophilus, Enterococcus Faecium, Dried Spergillus niger, Dried Trichoderma longibrachiatum, Dried Basillus subtilis fermentation products.

Chapter Two: Consider the Culprits
Spot the Suspects Case File example

Chuck's food for his dog Bella is Kibbles and Bits Homestyle Grilled Beef Steak & Vegetable Flavor

Ingredients: Corn, Soybean Meal, Beef and Bone Meal, Ground Wheat, Animal Fat (BHA Used as a Preservative), Corn Syrup, Wheat Middlings, Water Sufficient for Processing, Animal Digest (Source of Grilled Flavor), Propylene Glycol, Salt, Hydrochloric Acid, Potassium Chloride, Beef, Caramel Color, Vegetable Blend (Peas, Carrots, and Green Beans), Sorbic Acid (Used as a Preservative), Sodium Carbonate, Minerals (Ferrous Sulfate, Zinc Oxide, Manganous Oxide, Copper Sulfate, Calcium Iodate, Sodium Selenite), Vitamins (Vitamin E Supplement, Vitamin A Supplement, Niacin Supplement, D-Calcium Pantothenate, Riboflavin Supplement, Pyridoxine Hydrochloride, Thiamine Mononitrate, Vitamin D3 Supplement, Folic Acid, Biotin, Vitamin B12 Supplement), Choline Chloride, Calcium Sulfate, Titanium Dioxide (Color), Yellow 5, Yellow 6, Wheat Flour, Red 40, BHA (Used as a Preservative), DL-Methionine, Blue 1.

Chapter Two: Consider the Culprits
Spot the Suspects Evidence Archive example

Deborah's new food is
Trader Joe's Premium Chicken & Rice dog food

Ingredients: Chicken Meal, Ground Brown Rice, Ground Rice, Ground Whole Wheat, Chicken Fat, Flax Seed, Herring Meal, Tomato Pomace, Alfalfa Meal, Dried Egg, Natural Flavoring, Brewers Yeast, Kelp, Lecithin, Salt, Dried Whey, Potassium Chloride, Rosemary and Sage Extract, Choline Chloride, Zinc Sulfate, Vitamin E Supplement, Zinc Amino Acid Complex, Vitamin B12 Supplement, Iron Amino Acid Complex, Niacin, Calcium Pantothenate, Ferrous Sulfate, Vitamin A Acetate, Pyridoxine Hydrochloride, Manganese Amino Acid Complex, Thiamine Mononitrate, Copper Sulfate, CopperAmino Acid Complex, Riboflavin, Manganese Oxide, Calcium Iodate, Vitamin D3 Supplement, Folic Acid, Sodium Selenite, Biotin.

Step 2, section 2 Case File example

Stephanie's food is Science Diet Advanced Care Original

Ingredients: Chicken, Whole Grain Wheat, Brewers Rice, Whole Grain Sorghum, Corn Gluten Meal, Whole Grain Corn, Chicken Meal, Chicken Liver Flavor, Pork Fat, Dried Beet Pulp, Soybean Oil, Lactic Acid, Flaxseed, Potassium Chloride, Iodized Salt, Choline Chloride, Calcium Carbonate, vitamins (Vitamin E Supplement, L-Ascorbyl-2-Polyphosphate (source of vitamin C), Niacin Supplement, Thiamine Mononitrate, Vitamin A Supplement, Calcium Pantothenate, Biotin, Vitamin B12 Supplement, Pyridoxine Hydrochloride, Riboflavin Supplement, Folic Acid, Vitamin D3 Supplement), minerals (Ferrous Sulfate, Zinc Oxide, Copper Sulfate, Manganous Oxide, Calcium Iodate, Sodium Selenite), Taurine,

Oat Fiber, Mixed Tocopherols for freshness, Phosphoric Acid, Beta-Carotene, Natural Flavors, Dried Apples, Dried Broccoli, Dried Carrots, Dried Cranberries, Dried Peas.

Chapter Two: Consider the Culprits
Splitting Section and Case File examples

The first food showing rice fractions is a hypothetical Ingredient List.

The second food, also used in the Case File for Ellen's food discussion in the shop was
Chef Michael's Oven Roasted Chicken Flavor

Ingredients: Chicken, Soybean Meal, Soy Flour, Animal Fat preserved with Mixed-Tocopherols (form of Vitamin E), Brewers Rice, Soy Protein Concentrate, Corn Gluten Meal, Ground Yellow Corn, Glycerin, Ground Wheat, Poultry By-Product Meal, Animal Digest, Oat Meal, Calcium Phosphate, Calcium Carbonate, Salt, Natural Oven Roasted Chicken Flavor, Potassium Chloride, Dried Peas, Dried Carrots, Sulfur, Vitamin E Supplement, Choline Chloride, Zinc Sulfate, Ferrous Sulfate, Niacin, L-Lysine Monohydrochloride, Manganese Sulfate, Vitamin A Supplement, Added Color (Yellow 5, Blue 2, Yellow 6, Red 40), Calcium Pantothenate, Thiamine Mononitrate, Copper Sulfate, Riboflavin Supplement, Vitamin B-12 Supplement, Pyridoxine Hydrochloride, Garlic Oil, Vitamin D-3 Supplement, Folic Acid, Menadione Sodium Bisulfite Complex (source of Vitamin K activity), Calcium Iodate, Biotin, Sodium Selenite.

Chapter 3: Engage the Hidden Players
Feeding Guidelines Case File and Evidence Archive examples

Natural Choice Chicken, Brown Rice & Oatmeal

Ingredients: Chicken, Chicken Meal, Whole Brown Rice, Brewers Rice, Rice Bran, Whole Grain Oatmeal, Chicken Fat (preserved with mixed Tocopherols), Natural Flavor, Pea Protein, Dried Plain Beet Pulp, Sunflower Oil (preserved with mixed Tocopherols), Soybean Oil (preserved with mixed Tocopherols), Potassium Chloride, Choline Chloride, DL-Methionine, Salt, Vitamin E Supplement, Zinc Sulfate, Niacin Supplement, L-Ascorbyl-2-Polyphosphate (source of Vitamin C), Calcium Pantothenate, Riboflavin Supplement (Vitamin B2), Pyridoxine Hydrochloride (Vitamin B6), Vitamin B12 Supplement, Copper Proteinate, Iron Proteinate, Selenium Yeast, Biotin, Manganese Proteinate, Vitamin A Supplement, Potassium Iodide, Thiamine Mononitrate (Vitamin B1), Vitamin D3 Supplement, Folic Acid, Rosemary Extract, Decaffeinated Green Tea Extract, Spearmint Extract.

Precise Chicken Meal & Rice Foundation

Ingredients: Chicken Meal, Ground Brown Rice, Rice Bran, Chicken Fat (preserved with Mixed Tocopherols and Ascorbyl Palmitate), Ground Oats, Beet Pulp, Flaxseed, Fish Meal, Chicken Cartilage (Source of Glucosamine and Chondroitin sulfate), Natural Chicken Flavor, Lecithin, Fish Oil, Potassium Chloride, Salt, Dicalcium Phosphate, Choline Chloride, Calcium Ascorbate (source of Vitamin C), Zinc Amino Acid Chelate, Iron Amino Acid Chelate, Dried Lactobacillus acidophilus Fermentation Product, Dried Enterococcus faecium Fermentation Product, Yucca Schidigera Extract, Biotin, Manganese Amino Acid Chelate, Cobalt Amino Acid Chelate, Calcium Carbonate, Vitamin E Supplement, Vitamin A Supplement, Calcium Pantothenate, Niacin, Pyridoxine Hydrochloride (B6), Thiamine Mononitrate (B1), Vitamin B12 Supplement, Vitamin D3 Supplement, Riboflavin Supplement, DL-Methionine, Copper Amino Acid Chelate, Selenium Yeast, Calcium Iodate.